Joanne Malley

Just Listen

to the Song of your Soul

Joanne Malley

SERENITY BOOKS

Editor: Patricia Florio

The author of this book does not dispense medical advice or prescribe the use of any technique as a form of treatment for physical, emotional, or medical problems without the advice of a physician, either directly or indirectly. The intent of the author is only to offer information of a general nature to help you in your quest for emotional and spiritual well-being. In the event you use any of the information in this book for yourself, which is your constitutional right, the author and the publisher assume no responsibility for your actions.

Printed in the United States of America.

ISBN# 978-0-9905815-2-9

Library of Congress-in-publication Data

Serenity **B**ooks
Publishing

www.serenitybookpublishing.com

serenitybookpublishing@aol.com

TABLE OF CONTENTS

ACKNOWLEDGMENTS

To my wonderful husband whose support and love has been unfailing in life as well as through the completion of this book. I thank him for the time spent on listening to my ideas and for his keen eye regarding the flow and consistency of this book.

To my beautiful children for allowing me to grow through my newest venture, even when my time took me away from them. They are my main purpose in life.

To my mother and father for their love, support and encouragement, and for always supporting my writing endeavors. They are the best parents a woman can ask for.

To my friend, Lisa, who eagerly awaited new parts of my manuscript to fuel her own beautiful soul and offered her unending belief in me.

To my friend, Wendy, for supporting my dream and helping to make it happen. I have been grateful to her as a writing mentor and thankful for our friendship through the years.

To various other friends, family members and acquaintances who supported me and gave me reason to keep writing.

To the professional talent of Serenity Books for putting my words into print.

And most of all, to my heavenly Father who has bestowed many beautiful blessings upon my life, including the gift of writing.

Dear Friend,

My desire is for this book is to help you find more of your own inner truth as you evolve into a better version of yourself.

Appreciate and embrace all that you are, and when you find your bright spots, confidently enhance them to a glimmering brilliance so that you shine for those meant to notice you. Pay attention to things you are uncomfortable with and polish them into a refined, more pleasing, enhanced expression of yourself.

Don't clench selfishly to what you have gained in life, but instead share your knowledge and gifts with others to help make this world a better place, where love can be a healing force to guide you to inner peace, and reassure you that you aren't alone when you are feeling displaced.

Follow me now, from the edge of the surf, as we experience the beauty and mysteries of the ocean as well as life's virtues and endless lessons.

"*Though the music plays, it's the lyrics of her soul that make her dance.*"

A Place to Call Home

We are called to the ocean when our heart and soul are already there.

The water's edge has a special way of calling weary hearts. I know, because the sounds of the tides have drawn me there for years – to unload life's burdens or rest under the healing rays of the sun.

Near the surf is where I go within to turn yesterday's heartache into tomorrow's hope and today's dreams into future realities. Everything pondered there is suddenly sorted or begins to make sense.

Fond memories always call me back to where clocks and responsibilities have no place. It's where my thoughts whirl, my spirit soars and where I write for countless hours to provide food for the soul. The ocean softens mind chatter and calms the spirit. I've always called it my peaceful place; my second home – where time seems to stand still; that is, until super storm Sandy hit in October 2012.

No matter where people lived, whether in New Jersey or elsewhere, the devastation was seen from everyone's living room sofa. The effects of the storm reminded me of times when life surprised me with a sneak attack from behind and I was left to settle my racing heartbeat and regroup. Nothing was the same after hurricane Sandy. It was heartbreaking and taught us all that life can change in a flash.

Though morale hit a severe low point, the generosity of many helped take the load off personal, structural and spiritual loss. Fundraisers, massive restoration efforts and helping hands ran the gamut of ways in which the heart and soul of our broken communities have risen above the destruction.

Art studios offered auctions and generous restaurants shared free food. People offered their hard work, love and support for those emotionally lost or physically spent. It must have stemmed from the most simplistic of life's virtues, which include hope for our future days and gratitude for present blessings. I relate because when I feel displaced and weak in the spirit all I want are caring arms around me and strong people to help me mend the pain. A comfort much like that is what the ocean offers me.

Regardless of the damage or how the tides destroy, the ocean, in all its glory, will remain vibrant and alive, something to be admired until the end of time. She is faithful to us and in our own faithfulness to her, we return for nourishment when led. Though she is a source to be reckoned with, she is also a source of life and beauty. And so, the only thing left to do after the storm was to restore every aspect of the coastline because we all know her worth.

I'm grateful that my peaceful place has been revitalized and that reaching the surf is once again as easy as walking across the sand and settling in, where my lap is my desk and my beach chair is my throne. On any given day I search for treasures, people watch or write. Many words penned there have become a personal gift, and hopefully a gift to others as well.

Those who love the ocean have their own relationship with her. The connection singularly and collectively provides personal restoration and peace in different ways to each heart. Where there's serenity and refreshment of the soul, there is often love and when love is evident, there's hope to restore all.

"*The greatest obstacle in life is often oneself.*"

My Journey of Depth

When on life's path, I look ahead for vision, behind for lessons and within for directions.

My connection and appreciation for the ocean became an affair that rooted and flourished over time. Its soul-drenching magnificence yet brazen arrogance is evident behind the strength of its waves and their ability to awaken and soothe my soul simultaneously. The personal meaning it now holds didn't exist during my first visit as a little girl since all it meant back then was playtime in the sun and sand. I've retrieved that memory often with joy and a smile.

It's easy to get lost in thought while there, and my connection is a special blessing where peace flows, wisdom emerges and the future is pondered with hope. It's where I dive into my heart, soul and mind and the depths of life instead of simply treading water aimlessly without purpose.

I receive and also purge through the private, subliminal conversations that are forever stored in the echoes of its waves. The same sounds, smells and visuals are offered at every visit and a generous amount of perfect wisdom is given without even asking. There's usually something different to learn about life or myself every time.

Connected through the music that seems to dance between our existences and where God's subtle nudge gently catches my attention, I tune into divinity. A special flow of life is created within while there as if God provides it all.

Ironically, hearing the ocean's thunderous voice offers enough inner silence to listen closely for disturbances that need to be settled. Without a doubt, there are countless others like me who sit upon its surf to receive a therapeutic touch when a tidal wave of emotions or heartfelt tears crash upon the sand when life becomes too much to bear.

Though a particular plan isn't always in place when visiting the beach, all that's required is to lie upon the sand, sit upon a jetty, or settle myself along the surf. All three induce quiet thoughts and a chance to contemplate; it's also a time to receive a dose of much-needed restoration. Long walks are so appealing, as I never know what treasures will end up at my feet as the tide rolls in. Even the broken shells offer food for thought as they have gone through quite a journey to end up in pieces, much like I sometimes have through life's challenges.

As the battered pieces are cast back into the water, they offer insight into what they could mean. They mirror exactly what happens during difficult times when I feel confused, mixed up or shattered like a heap of broken shards.

My life has been about evolution and I've tirelessly attempted to repair my cracks. But those cracks and imperfections served as a necessary reminder of how far I've come and why they were received in the first place.

They are the spaces filled and strengthened by divine intervention and by the gentle bond of love offered by the special people in my life. Both have helped repair some of the damaged parts incurred through the years and evidence of the flaws and personal pain are reminders that I'm human with frailties, vulnerabilities and faults like everyone else.

When I find a flawless sand dollar or pristine shell, they're a reminder that I've been given many perfect little blessings along the way and there's a choice about what to focus on in life. Brokenness is a necessary route to new awareness and it often leads to life's gifts that keep me going.

There are times to acknowledge the broken shells and times to focus on the perfect pearls. At any given moment, whether life is seen as damaged bits and parts or as beautiful as an oyster's gift, one thing is for sure; life has a way of evening out the score.

My depth rivals that of the ocean because living on the surface is not for me. I'd rather be at the bottom of life's sea sifting through my treasure chest where special jewels await me. In the depths is where I often linger to receive more of what I crave.

I relate to the mythical belief about mermaids and lightly joke about being one as Anais Nin so eloquently stated in her quote, "I must be a mermaid for I have no fear of depths and a great fear of shallow living." It's no wonder I return continuously to retrieve what's rightfully mine in order to make the most of what life has to offer. Luckily, I know exactly where to find those jewels of wisdom inside of me, so they can be applied at the perfect times in my life.

Each person has an ocean of wisdom inside as well. The key is to find it, retrieve it and let it rush into the barren parts that need to be awakened or filled. Divine wisdom reveals the truth to each one of us in a personal way if we consciously look to find it.

Not all jewels of experience and wisdom in life sparkle, but certain ones have found their way into my possession. These little gems, though sometimes embedded with occasional struggle or pain, help me to live out life's lessons and rise to a place of higher understanding and appreciation. Even the dullest jewels of wisdom with no apparent beauty reveal their meaning along the way, as the experiences gained while noticing them appear refined to a glimmering luster and are rendered priceless to my life.

The more receptive I am, the more my inner voice can be heard. Listening to my authentic self is an undeniable understanding with very few doubts, but only if I'm honest with myself. In order to improve or change my life where needed, I must not only listen, but act upon that voice and embrace it, even when I don't like what it says. Sometimes, discomfort arises when the truth is revealed and I know that's a place in need of my attention.

Now that I know exactly who I am, my walk in life suddenly took on new meaning. My purpose has become as clear as the refreshing water I wade in at the shoreline. I believe I'm meant to be a writer and encourager and find it second nature to do both. I've also learned my gifts and talents are not solely meant for me, but are to be shared with others in the same way the gifts of others aid in my own life.

It's sometimes necessary to take off my life jacket to be pummeled by a few of life's unexpected waves. Times of struggle reveal what I'm made of and my soft exterior hides a tough, strong side well. I've had to trust my own faith and resources while getting extremely soaked amidst the choices made, consequences endured and the many difficult times encountered.

It's been a blessing to have quite a few people waiting along the surf with a symbolic blanket and a hug offering the love, security and warmth needed to carry on. Also standing there, were a few who lovingly threw me back into the swirling waters of life to gain more determination or strength for what was yet to come. They must have sensed that my challenge wasn't over. I thank them all because they delivered the type of love needed at the most appropriate times.

Tough love offers many lessons and God also threw me back into the rough seas for reasons beyond my knowledge. He watched me paddle, ensured I stayed afloat, and then offered his hand for rescue from the tumultuous waters. He knew afterward that I'd emerge more resourceful and courageous for what lay ahead.

Though being guided to wholeness, I may still make many mistakes along the way and there's no doubt disappointment will sometimes arise. Despite the wrong turns, the lit path always calls me back through divine leadings and I know it will continue to do so.

I've curbed the use of regret as some choices later deemed unwise have offered new awareness, a fresh outlook or priceless knowledge in the end. Luckily, God makes allowances for human nature and forgives me for my mistakes anyway.

Through free will, my life can be changed where I see fit. Its paths are ever-changing, and I embrace the endless flow of circumstances that must be experienced with as much grace as possible.

It's apparent that my first visit to the beach as a young child remained a vivid memory for a reason. It repeatedly arose throughout the years, and I remained unaware of its particular purpose until it revealed a special meaning in later years.

I continue to look upon that time with a comfortable recollection of those sweet days gone by. And because it was only remembered as a day spent playing at the beach, any real meaning found beyond the sand would remain a piece of my future until its value could be deciphered and reflected upon.

I surmise that my destiny already knew I'd be called back to that place where diamonds appear to glisten on the peaks of its waves and I also sense God's voice beckoning me from beyond the horizon. It's as if His gentle nudge is intertwined with the words, "just listen" and there's no other choice but to do so. Being powerless to the cleansing effects of His presence and connecting to the song of my soul, I am rendered obedient.

The surf has become a place that has taught me free will enables me to be the captain of my life and master of the seas I sail. It's also where I gained the understanding of what fills my empty gaps. They will never be occupied by another person or materialistic distraction and only filled by myself and God's endless well of nourishment. My hope is that everyone finds that place inside as they do the same.

As I recollect my childhood memory again, I am seated in the back of the car on my way to the beach at Sandy Hook, New Jersey. Other cars whizzed by while the drone of traffic lulled me to a quiet place. My thighs stuck to the rear vinyl seat, where there was plenty of room for my small, impatient body to relax. I was quite young, because my little legs didn't reach over the edge and dangle. I starred at my white sandals wondering why it took so long to drive to where my sand toys would accompany me to have fun. I'm not sure if the suntan lotion in the small, brown bottle kept my legs stuck to the seat or if it was moisture from the hot, summer day, but its distinct scent has stayed with me as a fragrance I'll never forget.

I don't recall much else of that day, but remember sitting near the surf, digging to China like I do now with my mind's eye, because living on the surface has never been my favorite way to thrive.

As my little hands and shovel scraped away at the moist, gritty sand, I kept digging and digging, as if a treasure awaited me. To my surprise, a small crab emerged and made his way to the top. He quickly scurried away. Though startled, I continued to dig my way to China while my eyes followed his tiny body back to the water where he belonged.

That small creature was fortunate enough to innately know the place he must return to be completely nurtured. That memory became a symbolic revelation that in order to nourish myself, evolve or grow, I must go back to my source where my greatest needs are filled and also honor the leadings given while there.

He also showed me that although he shared the same space with countless other living things, they were all

12

distinctly different, had diverse needs, and required a place from which to obtain their life source, just as people do. His existence oddly mirrored mine regarding how very deep inside I go in order to thrive or survive. Once there, it's the place to be fully nourished, reassured and satisfied.

Without a doubt, God, will provide the exact wisdom deep within, but only if I pay close attention. It's a place I periodically find myself when humbled or broken, looking for answers or I require peace and healing for my journey back to wholeness. While there, I ask for my thirst to be quenched, my empty well to be replenished and the fire in my heart to be rekindled.

For me, source is God, the voice within and that alluring ocean he created. I wish every person guidance in knowing theirs, how to find it, keep it, and eventually embrace it as the place that takes them home to the inner knowledge of themselves.

I will only stop listening to the ocean when called to sleep on the billowy wings of an angel. It's then I will say, "thank you," to my heavenly Father for His guidance and meaningful journey. And in the end, perhaps my ashes will be cast into the sea to connect with God and His amazing natural wonder forever.

With a feeling of immense blessing, I'm grateful for that beautiful place on the sand where divine guidance speaks, the future can be pondered and my life can be reflected upon. It's where my feet want to dance, my soul can sing forever and I just listen.

Soul

The soul is the sacred essence of life.
Our body is a mere shell and its keeper.
The soul's energy enlightens those who remain aware.
Once revealed, its brilliance casts a glorious light onto others.
Its luminous edges have no boundaries and its growth is unlimited.
It has the power to awaken those asleep and stirs us beyond our
senses.
It is present in the greatest works of art, the most heartfelt music
and in things that render us speechless.
When entwined with another, there is an understanding of oneness,
familiarity and awe.
It sends tears to our eyes, hope to our hearts and beautiful thoughts
to our minds.
It has the power to keep us still or move us in ways beyond measure.
The beauty of the soul exceeds what words can define.
It is timeless, ageless and should be revered
The soul lives forever.

Uncovering and Revealing the Treasure

My life has shown the importance of going deep. For me, it's where much is uncovered and where the answers truly lie.

Though circumstances may send us flailing into the depths, we are often provided with the perfect recovery and growth as a reward for enduring the more difficult times we'd rather forget.

Life can steal our sense of self and strength, but it also provides us with plenty of joy. Our low points can be the birthplace of the high points and no matter how far we descend; the exuberant moments are reminders of how often we ascend to experience life in all its goodness.

I hope the following pages take you on a journey toward the true essence of yourself. Have confidence that nothing can break you unless you give away your power and everything you strive for can help you with who you wish to become.

As each life virtue and specific life challenge is introduced and expressed in the coming chapters, I don't wish to imply that your beliefs should be in line with mine, but hope there is much you relate to as you decipher in your own way what might help you through your life.

Please read on to absorb what speaks to you, and may your journey provide many meaningful steps toward the life you envision for yourself.

Joanne Malley

Self-Assurance

Don't Drift Beyond Yourself

You'll remain lost until you stop trying to find yourself in others.

"The modest star whispered to the radiant moon, "I wish my light was as brilliant and luminous as yours." The moon replied, "But I would love to be you and possess a gentle twinkling light that bounces off the night sky, for I have always wished my brilliance could also dance."

Much like a hermit crab, we retreat into our shells when confidence is lacking. Harsh opinions and criticism may lead to berating ourselves even more. Unfortunately, we may believe that we're unworthy of sharing our innermost parts for fear we won't be accepted or measure up to another. The nagging voice inside becomes our rival, and when we side with its negative tone, we become our own worst critic. That voice can be so strong it may convince us that we aren't special at all.

When we only look outside of ourselves, we miss all we've been given in our authenticity. However, who we are isn't only what we reveal. There's much we possess but reluctantly introduce because we might be fearful to cultivate, embrace or share it. What lies dormant simply waits for us to expose it.

If we keep looking elsewhere for our value, we'll continue to miss parts worth noticing. Wishing to be like someone else is futile and keeps us blinded to what we have because we're looking at what we want instead. Comparisons prove nothing but the differences between people. To embrace and share our separateness makes the world a more beautiful, interesting place.

The proof of diversity lay on the sand at every beach, where one can find a unique collection of shells admired for their own special characteristics, colors and beauty. It should be the same for us.

It's natural to see something appealing or different in another and want to possess it, but when we desire instead of admire, all the wishing in the world won't transform us into someone else. What we see in another is their light and special traits, not ours, and it should never stop us from becoming the best that we can be.

Sometimes, the very thing we want isn't meant for us. We are equipped with much of what's needed individually, with the exception of fine-tuning or improving our not-so-desirable parts for positive change or growth as we see fit.

I suppose picking ourselves apart might be of some value, but while doing so resist the urge to be critical and replace it with truthful observation and patience. Self-criticism leads to a detour in making specific changes. Personal change can offer rewards that make us feel as though we have transformed from a guppy into a great white whale with an enormous presence. Hopefully, after we see our transformation, we remember to check our ego at the door and only use it to remind ourselves how capable and special we are.

Many of us may have come to learn that the harsh, judgmental words of another are often spoken to undermine dreams and efforts or diminish our worth. Actions meant to impede efforts or destroy are usually created by those who feel envy, and they choose drama and chaos because their own life is out of balance. Their destructive nature can be a confidence killer and for those of us aware, we can see them coming as clear as day. When we do, diverting them becomes easier each time.

It's liberating to finally realize that self-worth is totally dependent on the value we personally place on it and not on another's opinion. The confidence we have in ourselves must be genuine or we'll never trust how capable or unique we really are. The more we try to be like another, the more we diminish our self-worth and miss the opportunity to become our best.

We should have no interest in shadowing another completely, but nurture ourselves in order to illuminate what shines most brightly. No matter how small we think our bright spots are, they can be cultivated to be much more. If we want to make a mark on this world, we have to make a mark on its people by stepping forward to show who we are, thus leaving an imprint on other people's lives and hearts.

If we continue to allow others to define us, it eliminates the joy of getting to know and accept ourselves. Our presence and special worth should speak for itself without having to seek acceptance or confirmation from anyone.

Feelings of self-assurance and fulfillment should emerge from the confidence we have gained independently and we should be assured that it already exists within ourselves.

Intertwined

One day beyond the pearly gates
the heart of God rejoiced,
another child would walk the earth
and this is what He voiced…

"My hands, like tools will mold your form
with threads of Heaven's fleece,
each stitch I make, each part I craft
reveals a masterpiece."

"Until you're born no one can see
the parts that I've combined,
and you will bear all that you need -
three pieces intertwined."

"The first – your heart, will beat with love
one's given every man,
though how you choose to nurture it
remains in your own hands."

"The next – your mind, will hold the thoughts
of what is right and true,
though what you do remains your choice
free will I give to you."

"The third – your soul, is empty 'til
you recognize I'm there,
it's then your being comes to life
and heaven sings this prayer…"

"It's with great pride we do proclaim

your fabric is elite,
exalted is the name of God
for He's made you complete."

"Who you'll become was meant to be
no other's quite the same,
He took the time to craft just one
and soon you'll have a name."

"He placed you in your mother's womb
and as you grew He beamed,
your every part turned out just right
exactly how He dreamed."

And, then the angels bowed to God
they praised His work that day,
He sat upon His splendid throne
and had these words to say…

"With hands like tools, I molded you
of heart and soul and mind,
creator and his masterpiece
forever intertwined."

Discernment

Ride the Wave of Insight

Divine wisdom is heard the loudest in the quiet of the soul.

To be at a place of confusion or crossroads can be more uncomfortable than sand between the toes. There's even more discomfort when an important decision needs to be made. We can beg, cry or ask a friend for advice. We can take another's opinion into consideration, but our divine sense should be consulted to carefully weigh the choices.

25

Clear discernment comes when we have the confidence to make intelligent, well-guided decisions by looking at not only our choices, but also the consequences. Experience and mistakes give us the insight we need to act accordingly and bypass any unnecessary, additional pitfalls in the future.

Hopefully, we aim to live in such a way that integrity, honesty and kindness is at the forefront and common sense and a realistic view remain important considerations in the decision making process. A conscious presence in our daily life helps us live it better with the intention of more than just surviving. Life without applying what has enlightened us is wasted wisdom and living without purpose is only mere existence.

Even though decisions are made with careful thought, we can still experience emotional challenges at a moment's notice. Undoubtedly, guidance through only our heart can produce much different resolutions than that of logical thought. What seems right at one particular time may not be right the next because of human nature and inconsistent moods. It may be wise to try to use both logic and emotions when deciphering our choices, but the fight between both is what creates difficulty in figuring out what to do. Balance is more suited in many areas of life.

We make decisions at our own risk and can be creatures of uncertainty. We're also fallible despite careful thought and only have our best efforts to give at any particular time. Floundering in uncertainty is a place none of us like to be. Sometimes, we're thrown into the fire. It happens to all of us who take on the challenge of awakening to a much higher level of understanding ourselves, others and life in general.

Oftentimes, we place ourselves in unfortunate predicaments because of our choices. We may consciously try to choose right from wrong, but life happens and we ultimately make mistakes – sometimes big ones. We're then faced with riding the wave of our blunders or wash up on shore to avoid an onslaught of additional waves.

After we brush ourselves off, hopefully our future decisions may be made with more clarity. If things sit right with us, we'll know because uncertainty, anxiety and fear will be as far away as the horizon. If it feels right with our soul, we know our decision is in line with our truth. It will always include our beliefs, which are often intellectual, moral, spiritual or religious. If we stray from that, we'll feel like our decisions were made while in another person's skin.

Oftentimes, we do nothing and hope for the best when in limbo. It's hard to think straight while our heart is breaking or our soul aches to be in a better place. There is no certainty in how long our situation will last or who can be trusted to save or steer us onto a different course. We try to figure out what to do or even rationalize our way out of our quandary, but the truth is no one can save us and rationalizing does not rectify anything.

Before hitting that wave of destruction, many of us know some decisions we make will pummel us like the power of a huge water swell. Despite that fact, there's sometimes a need to test the waters on scary, uncertain shores, even though we know we may possibly drown in our own mistakes. If this were the only consequence, we would rise up eventually, but in what shape? However, when mistakes are made, we sometimes take others down with us to drift along on a rough and tainted river, unnecessarily.

Thank goodness for the unforeseen and unexpected opportunities, experiences and lessons, for it's that personal wealth of knowledge and insight that we can draw upon to help us through future endeavors. Some of us have certainly screwed up enough times to learn more than a lesson or two.

As for many dilemmas in life, we can go to our inner well to clean up all the sludge that pollutes it. One has to be brave enough to whittle away at the confusion and chip off any previous worthless, dried debris. When we do so, it's easier to restore ourselves to a place where a better course of action can be taken to repair the damage, whether self-inflicted or not.

Then, there are those who aren't completely satisfied until they have traveled the seven seas and arrive at new destinations, collecting moments of thrill and mishaps, even if it appears to initially be a mistake – that's just how some people roll. But, even though this route may prove to be the misdirected way to the right outcome, it provides a lesson regardless, and we get better at perceiving and deciphering our choices. It's important to place value on the lessons and remember what they were as we embark on a path with our dignity and values intact. No matter how little gems of truth are gained, they'll draw us to an authentic life; the one we are meant to live.

With each step taken, we ensure more clarity and peace for the journey ahead knowing that the difficult route previously taken might be the road to avoid next time. Unfortunately, the same mistakes are often made time and time again even though most of us had the answers within us all along.

We have all walked different paths and have stood on various types of ground during our lives. Whether smooth, uneven or rocky, knowledge is eventually gained and bits of inner truth are visible along the way. We are wise to pay attention to what we've experienced and how it has affected and molded us. If we remain receptive, future decisions will be wiser. For those of us with religious faith, the voice might also be the one that offers love and guidance.

Be confident in who you become after lessons learned, and trust in where you are going. Just beyond the horizon, there you stand, as the person you were meant to be. Life ensures you will get there in the manner in which your destiny calls.

Love

Tsunami of Love

In that silent inner knowing is where one finds love.

"Come with me," said love, "to a place where words are not spoken nor hearts afraid to beat."

"But what if I am rejected?" asked fear.

"That's when you must allow courage to take your hand. It will offer trust and hope," replied assurance.

"But what if love leaves and does not search for me again?" asked uncertainty.

"Love will surely search for you again, but while you wait, share yours with another heart that needs it," said love, "and then it returns to you. For the circle of love never ends."

The deepest connection to another is in the absence of words - the place where our response to someone is effortless; an impulse that can't be controlled. Like two opposing magnetic forces, the attraction offers no invitation, just an inevitable connection, simply because we can't fight it. To pry ourselves away from love is as difficult as fighting the force of being pulled.

Love is an endless longing of the heart. It wants to share selflessly and settles upon us like the swift fury of the sea or sneaks in through a soothing whisper heard only by the heart. Regardless of how it initially touches us, love leaves evidence of its sweet embrace. It's desperate to be recognized and felt, and serves a divine purpose through the need to dance in all who treasure it, as well as in those brave enough to experience and nurture it.

We can't completely love another until we accept ourselves for who we are, including the unlovable parts, as self-love is the basis for all love. To love ourselves first reinforces that others are worthy of the same gift; to be loved without conditions. Complete self-love is a challenge because we are often feel undeserving.

Unconditional love doesn't wait for love to be returned. It has no agenda and no regrets while sharing it.

Its purpose is to shower it upon the ones we are drawn to for the simple privilege of loving them. It's eager to teach those who hold it how to give in its purest form. Until we know love at its core and that it wants no vice-like attachments, it can't be freely embraced between people. Patience and understanding of human nature allows us to see ourselves and others along with the imperfections, and enables us to embrace love simply for the joy of it without the excess demands.

For those who choose not to accept the love we offer, they make a decision on the leadings of their own heart and soul and it doesn't reflect upon our own worthiness. Those meant to be joined with us in life will do so fortuitously without the need to question or oppose its appearance in their life.

Though there are many types of love, its main purpose is to weave a thread through each human heart with an invisible connection. Love asks us to remain separate enough to bask in our own presence, while sharing our heart with another. Though they may not exactly beat in unison, the hearts that share love create their own special connection together.

As Khalil Gibran, Lebanese-American poet and writer said, "Let there be spaces in your togetherness. And, let the winds of the heavens dance between you. Love one another, but make not a bond of love: let it rather be a moving sea between the shores of your souls."

To love someone, yet allow them freedom in the love you give, is a difficult concept to learn and grasp. Love nurtures and allows freedom and doesn't seek to own or control. A love that hungers to control is an insecure love afraid of loss. Loving this way may force it to leave because it doesn't want to be manipulated in any way. It's a natural reaction to want to cling, but it interferes with the freedom each person needs to grow separately and also together for a healthy, balanced union.

Love refuses to be held back, yet often battles the chains of restraint by those afraid to experience it. It climbs walls and boundaries to embrace each special heart sought. Despite the fight endured, it prevails enough times to claim its place as one of the most passionate of all emotions.

It wishes to be caressed by souls that have released themselves of the need for selfish desires or egocentric plans. It mourns when abused and reaches immeasurable heights among those who embrace and cherish it.

Despite our desire to share our love for another, some are blocked from receiving it. Fear keeps love from entering the heart's chamber and it sometimes ensures its loss.

There are times we also let go of certain people because it's best to be separate for one reason or another despite the love we feel for them. Love does not necessarily die, but often chooses to hold another's heart in a different place as time passes, still aware of its gentle existence.

Trust that despite occasional loss, love has the capacity to visit us many times through our lives in many forms. It ministers to us in one way or another, and gently touches the tattered bits of our hearts. It finds us and flees, reinforces and soothes. No matter its purpose at any given time, we are stirred in a place where mystery, magic and healing thrive.

Perhaps the common symbol of love is a red rose because we feel as though its soft, silky petals have touched us in the place inside that only our hearts understand. We are to share it with those we encounter through life. Love should be held and cherished, yet released and sent to embrace another. Its ultimate goal is to ripple through the universe on a grand scale.

Love entwined with romance has a special way of leading hearts down a path of depth and intensity like no other. Side-swiped, spellbound and rarely warned of its intentions, we are often incapable of logical thought or sensible actions at its inception. Its power resembles a tsunami that grasps us in a relentless hold.

Its depth cannot be measured, nor can its meaning be easily explained. Words do little for the feelings evoked, and its magnitude of strength is hard to battle. Love can make us feel as though the stars in the night sky twinkle and shine only for us and our beloved. Where hearts merge and the connection grows in oneness, the cravings and hunger of love are sustained.

For certain, lust is never love, and often exists to fill a selfish desire. Love's only purpose is to love more. Lust's only purpose is to gain. Love's greatest pleasure is in giving freely; sometimes, even when we feel disregarded. Many have mistaken lust for love in confusion, and only when we look to the Divine for an example, can we know the true meaning.

True love does not hesitate to return it nor measure the amount given. Unfortunately, when ignored too long, the heart builds a barrier out of rejection and retreats until reassured that the love it seeks can be trusted.

Most mothers will admit that their love is given from an endless reserve, despite any interferences or challenges. There isn't much that impedes with the constant supply and flow of the nurturing protection it offers. Many different forms of love may try to compete, but the most genuine of all maternal forms will win the battle most often. Our children will always hold a piece of our heart forever.

In order to experience love of any kind, fear must not be present. One thing is guaranteed; love will change, mold and enhance our life. It will often tear us apart because of chaos that may surround it. However, love will always stroke our heart with the reminder that we're on this journey to respect, honor and share it.

A heart flutters at the thought of new love that comes its way. It experiences growth until it almost bursts, as well as laughs, learns, cries and most often, surrenders. In a special way, love gives security, offers hope and applies the most comforting salve to the human soul. It often swells from the sound of a child's laughter, beats in unison with a lover and protects the special people who have stolen our hearts. If we allow it, love will show us how to sacrifice ourselves for another without feeling we have lost a part of ourselves while doing so. When we share love, there is so much gain through what often blesses us in return.

When weaved in an unconditional fabric of goodness and truth, love shows no evidence of selfishness or arrogance. It desires an even exchange between hearts and will fiercely fight logic and common sense every time.

In order to experience its perfect gifts, the shield that sometimes guards it needs to be removed. Our generosity and vulnerability helps us experience the joy it brings as we watch another benefit from our gift of love.

Sometimes the journey of love, no matter what type, is not all divine splendor. Though beautiful like a perfect rose, we can also feel the swift prick of its sharp thorns through its loss. Though we may bleed profusely, there are often lessons to be learned. We don't emerge untouched, whether those lessons make us elated, disillusioned or broken.

The torment of any lost love can be so intense it rivals the passion that ensnared it. Disconnection from love makes the heart feel callously dissected and useless, as the heart's last breath appears imminent. When it oozes of anguish from its loss, it withdraws into a state of mourning, and retreats to nurture its wounds.

Many lost loves have been cried for onto pillows or strong shoulders throughout the centuries, but despite the possibility of our own broken heart, we know full well its responsibility is not only about guarding itself, but also about its growth. With that, comes the risk of inevitable pain. Walking on love's hallowed ground is a chance we all take, and our hearts are ultimately at the mercy of the ones we trust with it.

The heart is designed to break and mend, though not always eager to embrace new love. The memory of pain often keeps it closed. There's nothing more difficult than allowing love to flow in and through us, not knowing what course it will take. Hearts are resilient and have no limits, but neither do their ability to feel abused or broken. In order to move past the fear of additional pain, love should eventually be embraced again or we'll remain closed off to all we wish to experience.

The heart is also known for sensitivity and repeatedly tries to shield itself from being damaged and hurt. It remembers the grievous work required to stitch its holes and stop the bleeding when ripped apart. Luckily, we often find solace in the fact that reinforcement can arrive through the love of another soul, but only if we don't push it away through fear of it eluding us once again. For every heart that's drowning in sorrow is the hope of a willing heart to show comfort.

Through its memory of pain, a wounded heart can become a stronger heart – one that can comfort another because of the lessons learned. For those who have experienced much loss, trusting in love's gifts is often enough to lean on for renewed hope.

To know the heart's sensitivities should remind us to take special care whenever we hold one; for it will touch us and teach us in ways beyond measure, while presenting us with a priceless gift. To destroy one is to ruin the most precious portal able to send or receive love to another.

The heart beats to the rhythm of its own truth and gains a collection of beautiful melodies with each special experience. It replays the tunes to keep the love alive or erases the music to forget the pain it has endured.

We all have memories that lay deep within us regarding how our hearts have lost, endured and loved...all for the blessing to know and treasure its beautiful offering. There may be some that have traveled along our path and touched our heart in such a way its fibers are forever changed.

As it beats until the end of time, moments continue to pass, and memories of the mind fade, but the heart will always remember. In its chamber of pleasant dreams and reflection, the flawless melody that love sings plays an endearing tune forever.

Peace

Immersed in Peaceful Waters

Where you find inner peace is where your soul finds its home.

F inding peace within ourselves and amongst others is integral for happiness, balance and well-being. Unfortunately, it can elude us for a number of reasons including daily nuisances that are bound to steal our joy. Refusing to allow negative circumstances or people to rob us offers a better chance of finding and keeping it.

Life isn't perfect, and many days present troubles and challenges. But peace starts within us despite what's happening around us, and we're often responsible for destroying our own balance.

If our days are lived as they unfold instead of retrieving those already gone or reaching for those yet to come, we lessen distractions and can stay more in the moment. Long-term solace isn't found in either place, especially through unfavorable thoughts or situations that keep us there. Only we can move past what's uncomfortable and changing anything is always up to us.

Peace isn't only obtained by adding positive things to our daily lives, but also by eliminating the negatives such as anger, fear and worry which block our way to having it. The helpful things we choose to do for our benefit serve no purpose until negative things are lessened or eliminated, if possible. Then, we're able to get a better grasp on things the way they are and change them for the better.

It's also important to be realistic and know that despite our greatest efforts, we're living an imperfect experience and there are times we'll feel emotional disturbance and imbalance. Though uncomfortable, it might be wise to sit with those emotions, ponder their meanings, and accept them for what they are for the time being. When we become familiar with the feelings that stir, we realize that many times there isn't much to fear about them. The good thing is, everything will pass and the place where we are at any given moment isn't the place we'll stay. What a relief to know that time changes everything; especially the things we don't like.

If we find what we love about our life and concentrate on them we'll see little blessings that make us smile or reflect upon a time when we felt comfortable in our world. When we focus on positive things, we relax more and reduce anxiety.

Each new day offers another chance to shed what keeps us from peace. We have the power to recreate our world despite any situation we are currently in. We can choose exactly how we wish to feel and trade our restlessness for security, and our upheaval for order through our thoughts and positive actions.

What can we do to ignore the thoughts that stir anxiety, stress and fear? It makes sense to choose ones that create a relaxing state of mind. Though there can be difficulty in changing our patterns, what the mind believes is often true for us. If our thoughts create what we believe, it makes more sense to foster those that are uplifting and healing. Time and patience is required to create a new pattern of positive thinking and living, but to feel the change there has to be a change.

So many healing modalities are available to us all such as yoga and meditation. Public groups exist so we can include ourselves in on the latest techniques. The amount of help available is limitless with our technological highway as well. If we stand still, we are only guaranteed to stay exactly where we are.

When we're empowered and capable, we're naturally more at peace. Our anxiety begins from our thoughts, and finding a way to change our mindset often alters our circumstances. In the process, we can also change ourselves. A new perspective can mean different perception and then much more is possible. Setbacks and emotions will always be apparent, but these factors are temporary and there are choices regarding how to incorporate a peaceful balance.

We don't necessarily find peace; it's created in the company we keep, jobs held and the daily living patterns adhered to. Those who have peace in their lives consciously create it by what they allow. Others are afraid of change or action and are sometimes to blame for their lack of peace. Old habits give us much of the same; new habits create different options and opportunities.

There's a serene place in the quiet solitude of our souls. It's where the stillness of heart, mind and spirit can be embraced in the silence. If we listen closely, we are called to nestle with and experience peace from exactly where we are.

Joanne Malley

Vision

Look Beyond the Horizon

Wisdom is what we gain when our blindness becomes sight.

Being able to see is a blessing and the gifts we've been given through sight should never be taken for granted. Our eyes not only let us see our surroundings, but they teach us to learn and experience life in all its wonder. Whether witnessing the birth of a child, capturing a perfect sunset or taking in the endless beauty of our world, we remain eager to keep looking.

Finely tuned vision raises our awareness to a higher level of complexity and when our sight improves to include more than merely seeing ourselves or what is directly in front of our eyes, it will provide us with deeper perception.

In order to rise above and beyond where we are at any particular moment, it's beneficial to hear, see and feel with depth. We can do all three from within, where we should listen, not only hear, that familiar voice we sometimes ignore. Hearing and listening is much like the difference between sight and vision. The clearest vision is a three-dimensional look into our souls instead of the shallow, one-dimensional empty glance blurry vision usually offers at the surface.

Being able to view ourselves objectively is one benefit of seeing clearly. However, it's much easier to uncover the faults and shortcomings of others than it is to uncover them for ourselves. Clarity may be delayed or come at the most inopportune time, but the goal is to help us see what's most needed for our benefit.

"The best teachers are those who show you where to look, but don't tell you what to see," says Alexandra K. Trenfor. Some people have a better view and can point us in the direction leading to our own improvement. To be able to notice our faults, without the insecurity that often goes along with it, gives us the perfect chance to reveal and improve upon the enhanced version of ourselves.

Through being more open minded, we can do away with blind stubbornness. Never discount the eyes of another, for they have come to see things that may be meant for our own eyes someday.

Some people don't realize the depth at which they can also see with their heart as well as their soul. When our vision is improved enough to include what's felt from within, we are offered the best view of the human spirit.

Greater depth gives us the ability to find the real treasures in ourselves, others and life in general. It's meant to enlighten us spiritually as it helps us to view the external world and internal spiritual world even better.

When we realize the beauty that can be retrieved from the depths of our earth and sea, like the diamonds and pearls we harvest, it is evidence that the same is true for ourselves. More of life can be witnessed and enjoyed when we become a deep-sea diver rather than a surface dweller.

Sharp and receptive vision helps us to see things we've never seen before. Our eyes suddenly remain more open than closed. When finely tuned with a good measure of depth, discernment and perception they magnifiy beauty and promise where others don't see it; to see hope in the shadows and love in the unlovable. Suddenly, we know where to look and we wonder how we previously missed what has become so obvious.

Another type of vision we can count on is hindsight. It's there for a reason – to reflect back on life in order to gain wisdom, clarity and certainty and not second-guess what we see regarding future situations. What was once accepted out of our own ignorance, blindness or vulnerability can now be rejected because of new wisdom. The newly found clarity received will lead to a brighter path along the way.

Hindsight is available whenever we need to reflect upon our experiences and lessons or use them for guidance. Reflection can return a gift that keeps on giving in our future endeavors when we see things without a veil of lies. Illusions are often destroyed when we listen to the truth that we didn't originally want to hear. The more illusions we uncover, the closer we come to embrace what really is.

We can also see through our dreams, our hopes and our goals. Sight that is embellished with all three enables us to make them more of a reality, as long as we blend them with a healthy, reasonable dose of honesty and desires that we know are attainable.

Once we trust our vision more, we may feel secure enough remove those rose-colored glasses often used. They make everything look beautiful and rosy, but the truth serves us better when viewing people as well as our circumstances and our world. Wisdom is received through learning, and it happens only with eyes wide open without a lens that's tinted with misconceptions or lies.

For each person, rose-colored glasses are a different size, shape and tint. Some people choose to see the world while always wearing them. The pain of seeing everything in its truth can be uncomfortable, or even unbearable, especially when the truths are about us or something that personally affects us.

Ignoring what we see is the easy choice and many of the undiscovered truths make us run the other way once revealed. It's human nature to guard ourselves, but to remove the protective lens is more effective. If we leave on the glasses, we stay in the same place wishing we could live instead of viewing life through restrictions that might prove to be dangerous.

Others seldom wear their rose-colored glasses, as they are beginning to see distortions and are brave enough to notice and admit exactly what they are viewing.

For those who have removed them totally, their focus is on a clear view and they're not afraid of the truth. For in truth there is freedom, and freedom gives us the ability to discard what is unnecessary and untrue. They embrace life for every step and have no time for fabricated lies or illusions.

Clear vision ensures a certain measure of peace and happiness in our lives. We can plan ahead with hope or focus on the pain of the past. We can see the best in people instead of looking for the worst. It's our choice, but with our soul-inspired eyes intact, the past and present can be seen exactly as they should be.

Joanne Malley

Happiness

Destination Happiness

Let reality take you toward joy.

N o doubt we all want to be happy, but it's not a
place to seek, nor a thing to find. It's a state of
mind released from the inside. Happiness is
often overlooked and not recognized as
something that's always there underneath it all. It's visible
in small morsels and snippets of life's moments, yet many
expect it to arrive through an enormous event or drastic
change in their current life.

Unrealistic expectations and dreams, a shift from the mundane or designer incidentals, won't bring us what we search for. Some waste their time on borrowed slices of happiness from their wildest dreams and are eventually disillusioned by all that never becomes a reality.

And while some continue to sow endless pleasures from unrealistic goals and accomplishments, valuable time is wasted in a land with other dreamers. Instead, we should take a better look at the valuable elements that life has provided right before us. Sometimes the smallest blessings and tidbits of life awaken us to what we have instead of what we lack.

When we embrace the special moments that present themselves and appreciate them as they arise, happiness is nothing to look for after all; it just seems to show up because it was there already. The smallest blessings can bring simplistic joy and gratitude leading to a much happier life.

A happy state of mind can be found in the stillness, the rustling of leaves, the melodies of birds and in the sound of laughter. It can be felt in skin touching skin, lips touching lips and souls touching souls. It's apparent in many things, but perhaps we neglect to see them because we wait for something grand to awaken us to it. If we build upon our joy by starting small, to our surprise, we'll be closer to those dreams of grandeur that are produced by what lay in our heart instead of what we wish to attain.

Happiness isn't found in any person, place or thing and materialistic possessions only provide a temporary high. No one is responsible for our state of happiness but us. Another cannot provide it nor take it away, and the quickest, surest way to poison it is to give that power to someone else.

We can also delight in the reflection of our special memories that tug at the heart of our most treasured moments. They may be forever gone from our grasp, but will always remain alive through the breath of life we give them as we recall them one by one. We can revisit them anytime and also temporarily send them away after we feel refreshed enough to carry on again in the present. Joyful memories will always remain little treasures through our lifetime.

We either realize where our happiness truly resides, which is in the intangible gifts of life or through special isolated moments on a daily basis, or we'll plunge deeper into a cavernous dreamland where we just keep fishing in a shallow river retrieving nothing.

Life offers many circumstances that create an imbalance in us physically, emotionally, spiritually or mentally. Many predicaments remain out of our control, but there are times we're the ones responsible for making ourselves miserable. There are also times life can't deliver large doses of happiness since our daily existence is never perfect. No matter how much we try, we simply can't continually muster the energy or strength to keep up with the façade of falsely manufactured happiness.

We may also continue to sabotage our chance at happiness through our self-defeating inner dialog, negative habits or focusing on undesirable things. We also diminish it when we concentrate on what takes our pleasure away.

If we avoid the negatives and concentrate on the positives, the chance of being in a better place materializes. Keeping a conscious record of our blessings reveals more reasons to be happy about life. When we see how much we have, there's less to look for and desire.

Happiness can be as simple as feeling the grains of sand beneath our feet because it means frolicking without responsibilities to ponder. Or, it can mean holding a newborn as we contemplate innocence and recall our own youth. It can even find us at the tail end of life's trials simply because we survived. True happiness means many things to many people, but it garners the same end result; joy in our heart and gratitude for experiencing it.

When we remember what it's like to be unhappy, we're more apt to help others who need to be uplifted in their time of need. To acknowledge and partake in another's happiness is an easy way to spread the joy and perhaps catch a smile to elevate our own state of mind. We also have the power to foster a bit of happiness in the lives of others through our words or actions, which hopefully spurs repetitive acts of kindness.

We all have the right to be happy in the place we are. We should never feel a need to have to earn it nor should we resist it through the undeserving attitude we create for ourselves out of unworthiness or guilt. Self-punishment is not only a detriment to ourselves, but to those around us and does nothing to help us experience the things we deserve and desire most. Self-defeating thoughts create a barrier that makes it harder for happiness to penetrate and settle in our lives while making it more difficult for us to share it with others.

Life isn't about getting to the finish line where the prize is wrapped in a perfect box. It's about embracing the little moments of joy that present themselves along the way and finding the beauty or lesson in all of them.

The road to contentment is closer than we think; yet only limited by our thoughts. Be fed by seeking riches of the heart and soul and of all that is inside, as the wealth offered by the world holds no lasting value.

Like the glasses we look to find though they are on the bridge of our nose, happiness is as close as we are in the moment. It's simply a state of mind we are meant to create for ourselves through the blessings, experiences and memories that reveal themselves through a grateful heart.

Forgiveness

An Act of Grace

The scariest prison is the one we place ourselves in.

When we don't forgive, any one of us can end up in an emotional prison. Though not always obvious, our refusal to forgive others may haunt us, sometimes in destructive ways, despite a slow perish inside the barriers of our chosen demise. We are equally distressed for the grace we haven't been shown when we wish to receive it from another, and even more taunted if we refuse to forgive ourselves.

Withheld forgiveness that's deserved often suppresses compassion and love, which are the very things we seek for ourselves. Our offering only requires us to be humble; even if it's at a time we don't see, understand or relate. Though we may not agree to our wrongdoing, an open mind and a willing heart to communicate differences or points of view can lead to peace with another in a strained situation.

If our actions have hurt someone enough to cause distress, even if unintentional, recognizing that fact should be enough to at least acknowledge it. It's a generous gesture to extend the exact graces we think we deserve for ourselves, as we all have less than stellar life performances we'd rather forget.

What should we do when we don't feel the need to apologize? There are plenty of times we have the right to stand firm in our stance that we're not guilty of wrongdoing. Perhaps, we need to realize that an apology for hurting someone, even if unintentional, is not necessarily an admittance of guilt, but an offering of understanding to help ease discord with another, simply because we'd like to receive the same gift for ourselves.

As Rumi, a 13th century Persian poet reveals, "Be like the sun for grace and mercy, be like the night to cover other's faults, be like running water for generosity, be like death for rage and anger, and be like earth for modesty." Long ago, this wise poet already discovered some keys to forgiveness in a very metaphoric way.

Reluctance or refusal to forgive can interfere with seeing or enjoying the present blessings of today. It manages to keep us locked into distress and strained relationships. There's no future in bad memories or negative feelings that continue to surface through the unwillingness to forgive, whether we should've extended it or received it.

If we're the recipient waiting for an apology we never got, we need to learn that hearing the words, "I'm sorry" aren't as important as finding the peace within ourselves to move past what we expect from another.

Non-forgiveness only keeps pain alive. It's like shackling ourselves to the bough of a broken boat to nowhere filled with decayed resentments, the stench of guilt and hurtful memories. That worthless trip only sets sail to a destination that can erode our emotional state, our lives and those who care for us.

Being humble is the surest way to bridge the gap between anger and forgiveness. Genuine humility enables us to not only apologize with sincerity, but gain important lessons from the forgiveness we extend. In doing so, we expand our capacity to reach beyond our former selves, limitations and egos.

It's human nature to expect forgiveness from others. Why is it so difficult for some to shower it upon someone even if their actions are unintentional? More so, why is it sometimes just as difficult to forgive ourselves for the mistakes we've made and the people we've hurt?

When we don't grant ourselves forgiveness, a vicious cycle of distress ensues and we withhold compassion and prolong our own pain. Perhaps we feel it's deserved, but the amount of self-erosion can be monumental. Any love we previously had for ourselves suffers greatly and so does our ability to function optimally.

In that place of mental torment, we dredge up the toxins of old wounds and previous assaults, whether inflicted or received. It is like a disease we keep feeding instead of starving the rampant, endless contamination of bitterness and anger that devours our core and also destroys everything in its path.

Despite the remorse felt, it's sometimes a challenge to move past the wrongdoing that caused us or someone else extreme anguish or guilt; especially those we love. In order to release both, accepting our imperfections and humanness and mending relations with others is an important start to new beginnings. Sometimes, by externalizing our pain, we inflict more of it upon ourselves or another in a destructive way. If we fail to forgive ourselves, we ensure unhappiness for the present moment as well as our future.

It's essential to release ourselves from our emotional prison; otherwise, we may drift into a dark place where distressing reminders gnaw at our chance of a productive, peaceful life. Inevitably, our future will include a trunk of baggage difficult to carry, though ironically, easy to attach to our backs.

When we're strong and generous enough to forgive, including ourselves, we're free to release the heavy load. Forgiveness isn't totally complete until we genuinely wish our offender peace from the depths of our soul and truly mean it. If the other person isn't receptive to our advances for whatever reason, we can always offer peace or closure from within ourselves and extend it to them privately so we can move on.

While we're at it, it's important to forgive ourselves for being foolish for allowing others to hurt us repeatedly. When someone refuses to correct their wrongdoings or apologize for them, it's often in our best interest to guard our well-being by separating ourselves from the person inflicting pain. Hopefully, our lesson learned will prevent any future foolishness. We can easily fall into this trap for people we love and even for ones that don't love us back.

In order to be fair with ourselves or others, eliminating anger as much as possible is a positive step, whether we direct it at ourselves or it's projected toward us. Anger keeps us from feeling any goodness at all and hinders our full restoration and healing. It resembles a rampant disease and once it takes hold it's hard to eliminate.

When the gift of forgiveness is given to us, accepting it with appreciation instead of poisoning or reopening old wounds offers a better route to healing. It's an insensitive act to repeatedly bring up earlier transgressions of another when the one who seeks your forgiveness is met with continual backlash. To repay pain with additional pain only sets another hurtful scenario in motion and the healing cycle can't begin. Do we want restored relationships and peace? What we do next determines what we'll get.

Forgiveness is one of the most special gifts to give or receive. It removes a heavy burden from our hearts, mends shattered souls and sets restoration in motion. Relationships become stronger when grace is generously offered and willingly received despite the damage that was originally caused.

To give or receive forgiveness is like erasing a debt that has burdened our hearts for too long. Unfortunately, we accrue interest on that debt in the amount of pain that continues to build. Whether we give or receive, it allows understanding and peace to filter into our hearts and helps to shower a cleansing love upon all involved.

Complete restoration is only possible when the light of forgiveness is much stronger than the darkness of condemnation; for it is the light that provides goodness and a genuine route toward love.

Simplicity

Pack a Lighter Life

In less we find more.

S ome people lead lives with a constant need for more while also keeping a hectic pace. Because of it, a time may come when a simpler life becomes more of a need than a want in order to stifle the chaos and create balance.

Who can continue daily living with an overbooked schedule or home life, and still juggle excess responsibilities, activities and stuff? Sooner or later, something has to give and when it does, we want to find ourselves on an island beach somewhere sipping a cocktail.

We continue to dream of a private nirvana. The bad news is that place doesn't exist. The good news is, we can still secure a better destination in life if we pack the essentials and leave most of the unnecessary excess behind.

Things of an insignificant nature are often temporal and can be attached to empty promises that only offer us immediate gratification or needless complications. In addition, what's foolishly sought can distract us from obtaining the simple spiritual food we require but sometimes overlook. These unnecessary things can tip the balance desperately needed in the wrong direction.

Obtaining more sometimes holds little value or purpose compared to the finer things in life. If we get down to basics and appreciate the meaning of life, we'd search and acquire things that add to our spirit more often, not our purse or status.

It may be that our search for more is actually an attempt to fill emptiness inside us or find replenishment, yet we look in the wrong places. Because of the careless choices we make, our spirits often shrink instead of expand.

A life encumbered by empty items, deeds or unnecessary fillers is much like an elegant woman in an overly-embellished dress. The complex design or dazzling jewels never make the woman more beautiful. In fact, too many gaudy details diminish her simplistic allure and value. It's the woman's aura and inner beauty that speak of her worth. Once the dress rips or no longer fits, what remains is her everlasting essence and the role of the dress only served as an outer shell.

An abundance of stuff and endless busyness may only provide a temporary fix for the wholeness we desire. It's like filling up on snacks instead of enjoying and savoring the main meal where the nutrients and substance hide.

Simple pleasures of the moment that often personally touch our heart, such as a glimpse of the night sky, a walk on the beach or meaningful book create a bit of beauty or peace from exactly where we are. They make us feel more satisfied because they don't fill a hole; they add nourishment that satisfies. There's nothing to tarnish and nothing to lose because the effects of what we've gained remain for as long as we choose to cherish them.

The same is true when an overabundance of life's entrapments and shallow desires are acquired and we expect them to enhance our lives for the better. When more value is placed on monetary or materialistic riches, we completely miss the gains from things that provide eternal worth. Transient pleasure is usually attached to anything that isn't everlasting and ensures emptiness in the long run.

A life lived more simplistically offers things that fill our spirit instead, as they become treasures of the heart. In doing so, simplicity and serenity can be found in less, and less of the right thing is actually more than having too much of what's eternally worthless.

Our lives are filled through where we place our focus. If we embrace things that produce emptiness as opposed to things that provide pure spiritual nourishment, the body, mind and soul react in ways to show us the difference.

We seek quiet moments in our busy life to find inner stillness. When our distractions are diminished, we reduce the external things that require too much attention or sap our precious time. External clutter equals internal turmoil. Excess anxiety impedes our ability to relax and enjoy life. When this happens it might be time to reassess why.

A cluttered mind can be much like an unorganized closet that makes us feel overwhelmed or out of control. When we figure out what to release, there is more room for new things of real importance and our life won't include a heap of trash, but a collection of timeless treasures.

Belief that we can achieve this is enough to start the change. It begins with casting the first piece of worthlessness overboard. From that point on, clearing out the stowed away junk becomes easier and we feel lighter and more appreciative of the spiritual gains we have collected. An abundance of senseless things will lose their appeal and we'll wonder why we ever sought them in the first place.

Most of us want more simplicity because we've come to believe or proven that less actually does provide more in finding the quietness within. When there is less to focus on there is more opportunity to bask in the silence, which breeds peace and balance and a spirit that thrives.

If we collected special moments the way we often collect stuff, there would be a surplus of blessings in the form of experiences and memories; all of which can never be tossed or replaced by some meaningless thing or new gadget we can acquire.

Simplicity is a process and a new train of thought for many. This change includes being able to live in ways that deliver the most gain. There's much more to life when the unnecessary time stealers and empty, worthless pursuits are reduced.

When too much time is wasted on fast-forwarding our moments in exchange for the next empty desire, we often miss what's right in front of us. The simpler things in life bring us closer to the tangible gifts that feed our heart and soul.

Though we may not be looking, the clock keeps ticking and passing moments cannot be retrieved. Simplicity has a grand purpose. It helps us keep better time.

Patience

Something Worth Waiting For

Patience leads to understanding, compassion and acceptance.

Much of our time in life is spent waiting for something. We wait for others, for relief, for things needed or desired, and most of all, we wait for patience.

The discomfort of losing it can be subtle at first and raises to a level of agitation. We know right away that it has arrived with its swift intention of setting off disturbance, annoyance and intolerance within us. It releases a slew of negative emotions; mostly unhealthy for us and those around us as frustration and anger rise.

The thoughts we have while we are experiencing frustration have a direct effect on how the moments that test us are handled. Negative inner dialog, outbursts or uncontrolled release of any kind does nothing to alleviate the challenging aspect of waiting, sometimes for longer than expected.

We lack patience because something hit a nerve or we have unrealistic expectations. Our way of thinking has a direct effect on how we handle the moments that cause intolerance. Though we often can't control the actual events we experience, we're capable of perceiving and handling them in better ways. Granted, our human emotions play out in a less than appropriate way at times, but learning to curtail them helps us in the end.

Our impatience sometimes shows us someone within ourselves we'd rather ignore, and the ones around us may choose to do the same. Each time impatience strikes, it gives us reason to look within to further understand our reaction and possibly consider a change within ourselves.

An emotional uproar or anxiety-provoked display won't help us deal with things effectively. Ignoring it certainly won't make it go away. An attitude of accepting where we are at that moment can help us move past unpleasant situations while gaining some composure. If we consciously recognize and embrace our indifference to a situation and just be with it, we can more easily find enough tolerance to move forward in uncomfortable circumstances.

Tolerance levels are directly related to how we perceive things. Sometimes, redirecting our thought process can help to see circumstances differently for our benefit instead of doing nothing while frustration gets the best of us.

For many of us, patience isn't something that's inherent. It's something we consciously and continually need to work on. It teaches us to tolerate and accept the unchangeable, enabling us to respond to experiences more effectively. Impatience stems from not getting our way. When we accept that life isn't always about us, we can conquer impatience more easily. Patience is more forthcoming when we release our ego more often and allow another person to be as important as we are.

We are most tested while waiting for someone else to act or do as we wish. It's such a wasted effort to think we can force something upon someone else or change them for our desired benefit. With this frame of mind, waiting is often futile and only causes more aggravation.

Though we can't always control the actual events of our lives, especially if we remain at the mercy of another, we decide how comfortable our wait will be. Instead of concentrating on what something isn't, the concentration should be on what it is and to find something positive, if at all possible. There are some things that are simply beyond our control and are meant to happen the way they do for good reason. Nothing is perfect or promised to always go smoothly. If we don't accept this, there will be inner conflict.

Life offers plenty of reasons for delay in collective ways. Long lines, automated phone systems, slow cashiers and traffic jams, just to name a few. These times can be used to get other things done or can serve as a necessary breather instead of becoming frustrated and riled. Our efforts may not always produce a successful result, but a conscious shift is a start.

No doubt most of us desire patience for unfinished business in our lives; emotional or otherwise, as very little happens at the pace we wish. Life can change our desired plans for an ultimate purpose; one we aren't necessarily aware of. In retrospect, we can look back on the course things have taken and see why they didn't transpire as quickly as we hoped.

Undoubtedly, there are times we're harsh and unforgiving of our own thoughts or actions and may also hold ourselves to higher personal standards. But if we aren't patient with ourselves, it will be more difficult to be patient with others.

On the positive side, resistance serves a purpose beyond our initial understanding. No growth or learning occurs through constant comfort. It's when we experience distress that we may have no other choice but to tune into some greater lesson or wisdom which doesn't always happen in our desired time frame.

Ralph Waldo Emerson's quote is simplistic yet difficult to embrace. "Adopt the pace of nature; her secret is patience." The lesson for our lives from nature is that despite stubborn impatience or wishful thinking, things are meant to happen at their own pace. The flower takes its time to bud, and when it finally does its beauty emerges peacefully, naturally and organically. It spreads its message of beauty and simplicity in its own time to all who are patient enough to hear and accept it.

It's helpful to remember that life requires a balance of giving and receiving and the understanding that what we wait upon isn't always easily controlled. The sooner we realize things don't always include our wishes, the easier it is to yield to what's happening. When that's the case, we hold the power over the situation instead of the situation having power over us.

If we believe patience has a purpose, we'll see that its goal is to help build our character and test our ability for silence while we wait. It gauges the depth of our resolve and edifies those who have risen to its challenge successfully.

The finest, most important things in life cannot be rushed. They happen in their own divine time without our interference. The situations that are disturbing teach us an important lesson regarding patience; to simply wait without expectation and have trust and faith.

Release

Loosen Your Grip and Let Go

The things we cling to may hold us back.

Wite-knuckled and tense, we may resist independence for many reasons. It's difficult to release whatever provides a sense of comfort and familiarity; like our first brave attempt at swimming in the ocean or family pool as a small child. Needless to say, we may have been terrified to detach from the one who taught us the skills to swim freely.

With uneasiness and apprehension, we felt thrust into unsettling moments when separated from our mother's hand and left to swim on our own. This is a scary experience; after all, most of us relied on our mother to ensure our comfort and safety on a daily basis through her loving, reassuring words and actions.

Having no choice but to muster our own independence, we may have thought, "How will I ever survive without her?" And so, the opposition and tears continued while we paddled and screamed, unable to trust.

Our imagination can get the best of us, but we rarely flounder in an ocean of famished piranhas with ferocious teeth as envisioned. Intrusive thoughts invade the mind and produce more insecurity or fear of being alone. Our fear only guarantees we'll remain stuck in the habit of dependence and insecurity, neither being the reason to endlessly cling.

When we set out on our own, there's never certainty, and nothing can be held tightly forever. Everything has its time to slip. The only certainty in life is that most things aren't certain. Wishing our life away waiting for the right time to gain trust is futile. We could be waiting forever.

Letting go of what no longer serves a purpose makes room for things that bring more freedom as well as the new things we're meant to embrace. A tight grasp on anything ensures that freedom will never be ours to experience anything new or fulfilling.

Newly found confidence in ourselves helps to ensure we not only make great choices, but ones that can recreate us. We can certainly ask for help, but the only way to grow without restrictions is to know we are capable and to do it for ourselves.

Despite what circumstances bring to any given moment, it's ok to let go simply because we're tired of holding on for one good reason or another. There may also be moments when we don't want to let go even though we realize it's best, as it may be something too special to replace.

Sometimes, we let go of what we thought something or someone should be in order to experience what it really is. It can only be done when we trade our expectations for acceptance, where the bigger picture can be seen or an entirely different one can be considered.

Certain people or situations may create a stronghold for us making it difficult to move forward in life. Our reliance on them, for whatever reason, often prevents us from detaching, keeping us bound for all the wrong reasons.

We've been given emotions to recognize, utilize and understand our lives and others. These emotions like fear, anger, sadness, disappointment and despair are there for a reason. They help us to notice pain and to recognize when something is very wrong. The indication is a sign that it might be time to let go when no other option seems viable.

Oftentimes, to stay attached is to be in denial and seeing the truth of another or a particular situation is painfully revealing. To squash the truth is to deny the feelings and nudges we receive for our best interest.

More often than not, we hold onto people or circumstances merely for what we wish they could be. Holding on out of unfulfilled desires or presumed needs serves no purpose. If we can't control it or its influences, acceptance is the only way to effectively let go. Habitual wishful thinking with no action only keeps us stuck.

And, then there are those who feel the need to let go of us, yet we don't feel the same. If we pay close attention, we can distinctly feel them widen the space between us or even close it off for good, though we do our best to ignore it. Finding the courage to accept the disconnection can be fraught with hesitance and laden with disappointment or even feelings of grief.

Unfortunately, this is just one more instance where we aren't in control. If it's acknowledged for what it is, in time we can move past the discomfort that ensues. Only an admission of powerlessness can bring peace to the situation we're in. If we close the connection and bid it farewell from our end as well, it'll be what it should be – the start of something more suited for the place we now occupy in life.

While in our retrospective mindset, many of us have realized that when we step away and look back from a distance at a particular individual or circumstance, we sometimes recognize that the cut-off was really the best gift we could have been given.

Occasional dependence is different than total reliance. We all need to feel connected to others in some way, however, with self-reliance, we can release things with more freedom and discard our restrictive beliefs and behaviors.

The manner in which we detach may play an important role in how disconnections in life are dealt with. If we let go by pushing someone away or ignoring a situation, we may not have the closure needed to move on with a comfortable sense of finality; as being in limbo can create anxiety or be emotionally painful for some.

When we release our connections or strongholds it resembles diving into chilly unfamiliar waters on a new journey to elsewhere. With no lifeguard or floating device, we are left to swim alone until we learn the best way to stay afloat. In order to diminish our fear, we need to let go, depend on our own survival tactics and trust that we can be self-reliant after all.

Self-preservation and inner security both come when we don't totally rely on anything or anyone to provide either for us. This is true of those who depend on harmful substances or habits to help them disconnect from life's extreme circumstances. Blessed are those who can release themselves of the bind that ensnares them as they move into freedom in their mind, heart and soul.

Equally important is the ability to release negative things we hold closely inside; like the inner voices that damage us on a daily basis as they speak in unloving tones. They do nothing but keep us in a vortex of self-defeats. We're the only ones that can break that cycle, despite how difficult it may be.

Our hearts know that we seek detachment from the things that hold us back, cause discomfort or keep us confused. Despite finding ourselves in the depths of uncertainty, we can slowly release all we don't need especially if there's much to question, yet little to embrace. Though uncertainty gnaws at us quite frequently, fate may lead us and wisdom eventually guides us enough to let go.

In the vulnerability of it all, we'll learn that we need to breathe slowly instead of hyperventilate, suffocate or drown in our unrest. When we find a place to just be in the moment and expect nothing, the nothingness eventually reveals clarity and peace.

It's often somewhere in the stillness of what's unfamiliar and uncomfortable that we muster a bit of confidence and are led to release and let go because that's all that is left to do. But, it can't be forced; we have to be ready. The more we do it, the easier it becomes. And with each necessary disconnection, we find a little more strength to carry on in our own confidence through the rest of our lives.

Truth

Uncover What Hides Beneath

Some of the worst lies are the ones we tell ourselves.

Denial is a detrimental bargaining tool used to keep us blinded to the truth we don't wish to see or embrace. We can only lift our veils and remove the earplugs if honesty and courage are present; otherwise, we remain blind and

84

resistant. To discard truth and wisdom meant for our growth only ensures we remain further away from our best selves and also disconnected from understanding others and vice versa.

Hopefully, we'll go about finding truth with open eyes to see and open ears to hear, whether we search for it on our own or find it through a teacher that life sends our way. No matter what is discovered, humility enables us to hear the stirrings of God and the voices of wise counsel. It's important to recognize the inner voice and nudges we feel since their purpose is to awaken us.

To notice the need for improvement may sear the ego, but taming it can be a positive step in embracing what we're meant to see. The wisdom gained fosters gratitude, as we realize it was only possible by remaining open and slightly vulnerable; two traits not always readily embraced.

For some of us, our beautiful parts are just as intimidating. When we discover a talent, desirable trait or a certain hidden mystery about ourselves, we may occasionally be required to share them with the world. Exposing ourselves can be like shedding layers of skin and revealing ourselves in the raw. We are then under the scrutiny of many and insecurity can set in.

What does our own truth look like and how do we uncover it?

Two things happen when we finally find our truth. We either want to shield our eyes and hide, or shout about our discovery from the rooftop to share it. When we are honest with ourselves and see things for what they are, we give ourselves a gift, especially if we embrace it.

It's important to realize that running from the truth won't stop it from chasing us. It's best measured with a healthy dose of logic as well as emotion and should never solely represent another's views, beliefs or feelings.

There are times the truth makes us retreat like a hermit crab, but hiding from the world like a pearl in a shell guarantees we conjure more lies in the safe place we created for ourselves. This place is most often built out of fear, blindness or even selfishness, but also exists because of love, understanding and compassion.

Our own truth is what separates us as individuals and we should reveal ourselves, not a false version. On the contrary, if we happen to see what we don't want to show, perhaps it's time to make a few positive changes in ourselves or in life's situations.

Shakespeare said, 'To thine own self be true." I wonder if he realized that finding it would be our greatest challenge. If we take this quote literally, we can cause much pain to others, especially those we love.

Egotistical needs and desires may be blinding and selfishness may surface in order to be true to ourselves. No matter what our truths are, if we act upon them they may cause pain in others because of impulses and actions we may not have fully examined.

Perhaps Shakespeare's quote implies that we find our real truth by knowing who we are at our core, taking into consideration our beliefs and opinions while securing our integrity and sensitivity. This mindset allows us to satisfy our desire to be who we are while allowing others to embrace us with trust.

Although bits of our truth can change daily in small ways, the character of a genuine person remains the same. And, even though decisions may be made with careful thought, emotional changes happen at a moment's notice and the wrong decision can be made. Something we deem to be right one day may be totally wrong for us the next because of our inconsistent moods, the leadings of logic and the interference of our heart.

How many mistakes do we make by living our truth? How many can be avoided? Life's truths are often life's mistakes, which can take us and others unnecessarily down a path we'd rather avoid. We should be careful that our truth of the moment does not distort the clarity of the mind, and hope that somewhere in the burrows of goodness and logic we do what our core beliefs suggest.

But, the certainties of the moment may not always be in vein if they temporarily steer us wrong; for afterward we may gain an enlightened spirit, a more open heart and soul and important lessons to help us travel a more in-depth journey. As life has it, wrong choices and detours usually provide more truth if we are willing to continue uncovering it and make the consequences right, if need be.

Despite our best efforts, there are times life's lessons are not learned while we walk within a perfectly charted path, and unfortunately, hurt and pain will ensue because of the things we need to learn and the way our particular road curves.

Living in untruth diminishes our personal power. Our truth is where we own our motives, intentions and actions. We must be sure they represent our authenticity. If not, we not only mislead others, but we mislead ourselves. When we're weakened in mind, body or spirit, we are burdened and unable to think or function optimally or authentically and tend to make the most mistakes.

If we walk a genuine path, we clearly see what dishonors all that speaks to us. In order to be connected to what lies within us, we must disconnect from what we don't relate to. Only then our truth is felt in our core.

It's to our own benefit when we expand within our consciousness, and that's never found in the beliefs of another, but in the inherent realities within ourselves.

Joanne Malley

Fear

Anchored to Dismay

Fear sits. Freedom flies.

Fear is real. When our safety or preservation is threatened by real danger, the heat rushes toward our throat, our pulse quickens and the fight or flight response activates. We naturally react to protect ourselves or loved ones from imminent danger. Whether we're non-confrontational or natural-born fighters, we all identify with the black hole of uncertainty and the reality of real threats.

Just as threatening are imagined fears, though they aren't a real outward risk. Regardless, they create trouble and imbalance in our well-being. In the silence of the unknown, we may hide like cowering children from imaginary villains with no names. We give them life and power and are certain the worst instead of the best will transpire.

Though there are times we plow through our fears regardless of the discomfort or insecurity we face, there are still plenty of times fear holds us back, restricts our growth or completely robs us in more ways than one.

Where we place our focus determines what we see and feel from the unexpected incidents in our lives. There is no validity to our imagined fears, but regardless, we create an onslaught of images that break through the protection we've put in place.

We are then met with a flurry of voracious hazards and risks that we willingly invite into our space. Many times there's no contest and no duel. The elements of our imagination infect our vulnerable parts, and the fight against fear becomes a battle we sometimes lose or choose not to face.

Once trickery and imagined scenarios are set in motion, it's very easy to feed them. Caught in their web, we often perpetuate their growth in massive proportions until doom overtakes us. We're then lucky to see the light through a pinhole of hope.

The internal chaos is just a fantasy in a battle that fiercely tries to prove otherwise. What are we really afraid

Just Listen to the Song of your Soul

of when we worry, squirm, tremble and sweat? For sure, we fear the disappearance of our strength and peace and are intimidated by uncertainties. But most of all, we are fearful of losing our control and being overtaken somehow.

When walls are built out of fear, we assume what comes our way is deemed to hurt, derail, or trick us. It's an uncomfortable place and the door of fear keeps us on the imprisoned side of the wall, where nothing can get in or out. Inside the barriers, these thoughts are emotional poison and keep us immobile.

Hearing the rest of the world live while we remain tethered and intimidated is a scary place and only guarantees our separation from experiencing life beyond the comfort zone.

Fear is created and driven by more of the same as we inadvertently execute our own scary cycle of living. It requires too much of our attention and in order to gain rational sense, we need to fight back with a vengeance. If we choose not to, we may experience the breakdown of inner peace and freedom.

Finding things to worry and lament over becomes easy but we should question the validity of those fears. More often than not, what has us bound and beleaguered is our own doing. Unfortunately, many things appear disastrous and we become an obsessive, willing victim.

Most of our irrational fears are born out of past experiences gone awry or out of totally fabricated lies we hear or tell ourselves. It helps to exchange the unfounded ones for thoughts that bring us closer to reality so we experience hope in overcoming it. When we focus on the process and steps we take a little at a time, we often gain a new outlook and a positive way of implementing change. We have to keep at it and believe we can conquer.

It's important to reveal our shield against fear and show up prepared for the fight. We aren't indestructible, yet we can be fiercely bold and capable. Every battle has its fighters and every outcome has its victor. Illogical fear is only imagined, so we have every good chance of conquering it.

Facing fear is never easy, but by allowing ourselves to experience and interact with it we get a better grip on handling the emotion, recognizing the power we give it and releasing its enslaving qualities. We see clearly what deserves our attention and concern and what's better left for the catastrophic movie scripts.

Fear is the place where we meet our own demons and facing them takes courage. When vulnerable, they reappear time and time again until we meet them head on and make peace with them. Though they often break us down, they don't have to rob everything from us. We can use their existence as a reminder that their appearance can be used to awaken us, help us change or become stronger.

We can face and conquer our strongholds no matter what they are, and imprisoning ourselves ceases when we refuse to wear the shackles. Nothing should be the keeper of our souls in the way that fear is. With fear, we remain committed to our comfort zones where nothing changes and everything stays the same.

Comfort zones are for repeating the same behaviors and moving beyond them is for change, where more fearlessness and assurance can be ours.

Gratitude

Finding the Gifts in Ordinary Moments

There is always a silver lining to be found.

In order to find gratitude in our heart, more awareness needs to be present so appreciation can take root. The spirit of thankfulness opens our hearts and helps us focus on all we have instead of what we don't have. Mindfulness ignites gratitude, which helps us celebrate life's moments for not only their actual blessings, but for the mere possibilities that can present themselves at any moment.

Gratitude offers a greater understanding of all we've been given and even what has yet to come our way. And although there may be times of lack, a spiritually mature person knows that they can still be accepting of the things they don't have for it may be in their best interest to not receive them at all.

Thankfulness can turn an ordinary moment into enormous joy, rain into relaxation and inconveniences into patience. When gratitude is embraced, we begin to receive much more by taking less for granted. Not everything in our lives needs to be picture perfect; for when we see beyond the pitfalls, there's so much more to be grateful for.

To receive blessings is the proof that they exist, but feeling gratitude for them is optional. If we don't acknowledge it we'll never experience it flowing into and through us, nor see how sending it back into the universe is what gives free-flowing power to paying it forward. Like a boomerang, gratitude sends giving into motion as it multiplies and also returns to us abundantly.

Gratitude serves as a tool for personal growth and a more abundant way of life. When we embrace it, we positively shift our current mood and help to attract more of the same to our days and lives in general. Recognition of our blessings should also stir us to share our abundance with others as well.

Despite our good intentions, there are times we fail to notice even the little blessings; especially when we believe our lives don't produce much to be thankful for. A grateful attitude opens the gateway to continual happiness from within and fosters a genuine appreciation for all that uplifts our lives, even in the smallest way.

Though it's easier to notice blessings that warm our heart, lift our mood and add outward abundance, the truly blessed are those who are enlightened through their hardships as well. They use them as reminders to be grateful for each experience, no matter what they entail and look for the little silver linings that are most often missed during the challenges. They see the blessings that brought them from the darkness into the light.

Though we may not initially see difficulties as an opportunity for thankfulness, an open mind and heart helps to awaken our occasional ungratefulness. By doing so, awareness is raised to the goodness that surrounds us because it highlights the blessings not previously obvious. Equally important is to trust that there are many good things yet to be revealed as each day passes and to be patient to receive them.

Gratitude knows that even though the stars in the night sky appear less than the evening before, the brilliance of the moon's emergence from beyond the clouds gives us evidence of hope. If we take notice more often, there are opportunities to see what's right about something rather than noticing what's wrong. This is where spiritual growth abounds and true gratitude emerges.

Just beyond the frightening shadows where the darkest moments attempt to destroy, is a place where spiritual prosperity awakens us to not only tolerate, but appreciate the pain, for we know that after the storm we are often gifted with the sun and a beautiful rainbow.

Where you find your challenges is where your strength appears. No one is strengthened in lovely meadows filled with beautiful fragrances. It's after a stormy night in the dark valley of decaying blooms when we tend to rejoice and gain much from the tears because they have turned into smiles of relief and gratitude.

Life is a very special gift. We are presented with it on the day we are born and it's returned the day we part. The time in between is not only for recognizing our blessings, but for appreciating them; hopefully, with much gratitude, love and generosity.

Surrender

Drop Your Sails

Ride with the wind.

Despite an attempt to orchestrate or control our circumstances, there are times we feel like surrendering; not out of weakness or defeat, but because there are forces in our lives working independent of our desire to control them. Seeking control does very little to offer answers or an outcome when one is not forthcoming.

Surrender is possible by letting go of the resistance we feel in a particular circumstance or when enmeshed in a negative way with another. It's like not wanting to swim any longer and realizing that we can float. What a great feeling to trust the water to keep us buoyant enough to relax. A calm, trusting attitude helps us realize there are times that doing nothing keeps us safely above water, regardless.

If we choose to wave the white flag, it has nothing to do with giving up, but everything to do with consciously giving in. It's when we let go of the outcome, hope for a feeling of weightlessness and accept what comes our way.

When clarity finally appears, there's a significant redirection because we can finally think straight. The cycle of futility has ended. It's possible that not actively being involved at all turns out to be a much better plan while we just be in the moment and trust. It's certainly a test of faith and a way to look at the unknown with less fear.

Surrender naturally happens when the mind, body or soul (or all three) get too tired of fighting. It allows life to happen on its own from a place of no expectations. We can still choose to trust even though we don't see a resolution. It's where the moments pass and we don't force ourselves to become involved. Things are simply what they are and what they will be.

Surrender allows us to be still despite the resistance or uncomfortable sensations felt. Not everything in life can be explained or provides a definitive outcome, but most things can be accepted if they are embraced as the only current option, which is sometimes the case.

To fight against surrender only ensures we once again get on a rollercoaster to nowhere, collecting more hopelessness, frustration, anger or even despair. It is ourselves we fight against while we perpetuate a battle from within.

Many of us have found that the more we try to control something, the more out of control we feel. Each time we submit control, there is an opportunity to release the person or burden that keeps us stuck. In doing so, we make room for peacemakers instead of peace thieves.

As we detach from unhealthy individuals or turbulent predicaments, we ensure self-preservation or find a new direction when answers temporarily elude us. Hopefully, stepping back will help us let go of the things that overwhelm, burden or keep us from moving forward.

Separation is protection from the battle inside that steals our power and will. Surrender also offers the kind of acceptance that can help distinguish between what we can change and what we can't. The real blessing is to know what their distinct differences are and act accordingly. Acceptance can transform us for the better; since that is where our courage and freedom is – the only place we can ever embrace true change.

If we are successful at reconciling these things, suddenly, not every battle is ours to fight. The ones worth fighting are those where the outcome can be changed with our best efforts.

On the contrary, there are many things we should never surrender; like our dreams or desires, for they are part of us. Our personal beliefs, morals or integrity should never be relinquished either; because they keep us on our true path and enable us to express ourselves exactly as we are. If any part of us is surrendered for the sake of others, we are being untrue. This only serves to hold us back from living an authentic life.

There are times we can't control the flow of life no matter how hard we try, but these are the times that require us to listen and go with the flow. Sometimes surrender feels like gain instead of loss and where letting go actually provides us with more peace and freedom than we expected.

Loss

When the Ship Leaves us Alone at the Port

Loss reveals our strength.

Nothing lasts forever. Life has a way of catching us unprepared when we lose something treasured and have to say goodbye - sometimes for good. Whether it's the loss of a loved one through death, a long, cherished relationship or even the disappearance of our own hope, if feels awful to be shattered into many pieces.

One day we're filled, the next day we're empty and sadness descends like a veil of hopelessness. We not only lose what was cherished, our sense of connectedness, comfort or abundance is taken by what suddenly disappeared. There never seems to be the perfect reason why loss should be acceptable and pretending that what's suddenly gone never existed doesn't work. Some losses are so devastating we wonder how we'll ever get past them and emerge a survivor.

Loss occurs many times through life and it's one of the hardest challenges to conquer. As if the actual loss isn't bad enough, we stand to lose more when experiencing it. We can lose our strength, our reserves, our vision and our will. The biggest loss through it all is that of ourselves. How does anyone recover from the wallowing and paralysis that buries us under life's biggest losses? It all seems unfair. Finding the light at the end of the tunnel seems futile because our eyes may remain shielded under a pile of anguish and misery.

No matter where we turn, the gaping hole seems monumental and is a reminder of what was. Though we're not necessarily alone in our loss, we certainly feel that way. Others who try to alleviate our pain may remain invisible to us regardless of their concern as we throw up our hands, cry out and ask for an explanation as to why.

In our emptiness, hollow, repetitive sounds rise from the confines of our soul. All of a sudden, there's nothing to hold for security and we're convinced the fullness of life is gone. It's like being lost in a dark room with no way of escape while we suffer alone.

The gaping holes in our pain-laden heart produce vulnerability and choosing what to fill them with should be considered with caution. If our choices are not healing in nature, we can end up even more forlorn or barren.

At times, we may find ourselves staving off the emptiness with empty things, harmful activities or careless, uncaring people. Poor choices regarding our healing can add to our spiritual undoing if what we fill ourselves with depletes our inner resources.

So much time and energy might be spent trying to ignore or forget the things we've lost, but it may be counterproductive as it can numb us to the gains that may be waiting for us. On the contrary, healing loss takes time and everyone's time table is different. Patience is necessary in the process of mourning any type of loss.

Loss and gain is often an even exchange in our lives. As one thing is taken, something else is given in its place with the passing of time. Though this does not replace what we once held dear, it can be a welcome distraction or a new beginning to something wonderful we never expected.

It's common that in our grief we try to soothe and pacify ourselves with either the beautiful things remembered about our loss or the lessons attached to it. Loss keeps us longing for something, which keeps us striving and living. This is where hope can be found again and the emptiness and pain is lessened. When the light at the end of the tunnel is revealed, our faith in life is restored and things don't seem as hopeless as they once were.

There are times the painful place is where we need to be in order to be healed, to move on and to feel fully alive again. Loss gives us time to become better acquainted with the silence, disconnection and pain so we can handle it better the next time it occurs in our lives. The silence is scary, but in time can offer a glimpse of light, which reveals a path to happier, new days ahead.

The reality of loss is that some things are going to hurt until it's time for the pain to lift. We're not mechanical people who can be summoned to dismiss the sadness or discomfort of loss, but we're capable of knowing the burden of loss will one day be lighter. Loss doesn't have to destroy us if we don't let it.

One way to hold onto the things we have is to cherish them in our hearts while we have them and allow them the freedom to leave as they are destined to. We can't stop certain things in life from parting. It's a hard pill to swallow, but this mindset ensures no clinging. We can still cherish and love whatever it is peacefully, knowing there's nothing to control no matter how hard we try.

On the flip side, when life is good, having and celebrating the great things also means there is a possibility of losing them. We may guard the things we hold dear with the strength of reinforced armor, but ironically, our fears about loss causes us to sabotage them in the fight to save them, especially with regard to relationships. Desperate or foolish actions may send our most cherished people packing because we stifle them.

We want to fully embrace what we have but sometimes we don't trust that our blessings are ours to keep. It may feel like our good fortune was meant for someone else and what we have will be snatched from us. Feelings of vulnerability or defeat may make us feel unworthy or undeserving of any goodness we hold and treasure.

The inner struggle with insecurity drives us to our own weakness instead of toward our strength and we inadvertently release what's been given before we have the chance to delight in it. Fear's unrelenting grip can be so detrimental it creates a vicious cycle of control, fear and loss.

One of the most certain realities in life is change, and in change there is often the uncomfortable experience of loss. Impermanence is a part of life and we'd better get used to it. It's hard not knowing what will transpire for us from one moment to the next, but just as loss will always cross our path, more often than not, something is added to fill the void in a new way, shape or form.

Sadly, there are many who have known more loss than they care to remember. They've learned to disconnect before connecting, shut down before experiencing and ignore for the sake of feeling less pain. Detachment is never the best resolve – it's the surest way to hide from life.

Living with loss is never easy. Sometimes we have trouble believing that the amount of pain we feel is even possible. So, what do we do? We either accept it or lose ourselves in it. Once we lose ourselves, loss has claimed its greatest victim. With a life ahead of us, none of us have time for that. Eventually, we need to get up and live.

Sometimes we close ourselves off when loss occurs. What is life if we refuse to feel love or connections simply because things may fall through our grasp? We may not realize that releasing something with an open hand and heart is just another opportunity to grasp for something else when we're ready. With 'goodbye,' there is sometimes a new 'hello.'

Though fearfulness and vulnerability are apparent through loss, we'll rise up again gradually and each step will reveal new hope. In loss we experience both our weaknesses and our strengths and the gradual gains reaped help ease our hurting hearts.

Restoration

Emerge a Survivor of the Wreckage

When we arise from the darkness we are often transformed.

We are born pure, simplistic beings with an innate desire to be loved, nurtured and protected. Our innocent selves often knew comfort, stability and surety through the early parts of our lives. Coddled from a place of warmth and love was where every need was met.

As we grew or reached adulthood, our lives may have been drastically affected by situations that disconnected us from our original security and roots. We may have been forced onto a different, more challenging path, either through unforeseen circumstances or foolish choices of our own.

After dealing with unwelcomed events, disturbances or turmoil, the peace we felt from our early days may seem like a distant memory when problems arise. Through times of imbalance, it's only natural to want normalcy again, which we remember as simplistic, little beings. Unfortunately, there may be times we consider doing just about anything to return to that place of complete peace and sometimes it can be destructive.

Life makes no promises, except that change happens quite often and our ability to adjust is tested. A sailor may know his course, but he also realizes the winds require him to shift the sails. When we are swiftly taken from our intended course, life circumstances change our alignment too, sometimes providing a much better way through unpleasant experiences.

Our challenges are often stepping stones toward the restoration we seek. Recovery and rebirth are opportunities that lead to improvement. Seeing the silver lining from inside the clouds might appear impossible, but the clouds eventually part for the light to shine.

Transformations often require a struggle and we sometimes endure defeats. Life proves that there are many events strong enough to knock us over and wash away our strength, such as when we experience a breakdown of security or watch the deterioration of things like our health, relationships or jobs.

With no warning, unrelenting storms may destroy parts of us, while leaving fragments of who we are floating in a sea of disarray or despair. At a moment's notice, we're left to wonder how to collect all the pieces and repair the damage.

If we're lucky, other survivors who have risen from their own rubble and ruins will support us. Some experience breakdowns and recoveries more often than others. Perhaps these souls are meant to be guides who have the tools to help others emerge from their own wreckage. Hopefully, they provide additional bits of wisdom to embrace.

Regardless of how difficult it may be to repair ourselves, we have the ability to evolve into a stronger version of ourselves, while leaving behind what simply should remain broken pieces. Not everything needs to be fixed and renewed. Some things are better left discarded for any number of reasons and we should hold onto hope when moving on.

Broken pieces may appear to be a loss and we may need to mourn and heal. Wisdom is to know what things are better left broken, move past them and look forward to wholeness. Our new, healthier state of being is what gives us certainty when we're finally ready to embrace it with the faith that all is well, regardless.

Too many of us hang onto at least one of those broken pieces for fear of moving forward; only to realize it does nothing but cut us with the broken shards, bleeding unnecessarily time and time again.

Our journey towards reconstruction offers endless possibilities. We are given the chance to build from a new place in our lives and include whichever parts are needed for our desired life with a new, blank canvas.

We emerge more capable to withstand any future waves of destruction that dare to knock us down. Freedom of choice always sets us on an individual path of greatness, but only if we choose to chase it on a healthy, sensible course.

It's a blessing to know that through our perseverance, we gain enough resilience to rebuild a much stronger foundation that's secure enough for each new step forward. We should start beyond our comfort zone for the greatest change where a better future awaits.

Some of us are responsible for stalling our healing when we fixate on those who've previously hurt us. We also may hesitate when we remember the pain of past circumstances. However, sometimes we're partly or fully responsible and must realize that despite the outcome, it's up to us to redirect. Our journey forward is often impeded when things like anger or a closed mind block the way to recovery of mind, body and spirit.

Unfortunately, feeling some level of pain and suffering may be necessary. Just like salt water on a wound, we need to apply the cleansing effects before we can be fully healed.

When we need sunshine, we often experience rain, and when it's finally sunny, we're still recovering from the storm. No matter which season, at some point, we'll be prepared to either endure or revel in the change. Our own perseverance and grace shows proof of our ability to stand in our own strength or sway with the winds that try to knock us down.

Collapse is never the end if we don't want it to be. After dusting off and steadying our stance, a new starting point can be the beginning of something great. Rumi, the 13th Century Persian poet states, "Where there is ruin, there is hope for treasure." He is right. We don't always realize what lies beneath the rubble of our lives. When we feel our time to give up has arrived, it's the perfect time to start over from scratch and rebuild from the inside out.

Our lives are often about restoration and rebirth. We have the power to acknowledge ourselves in our current condition for whatever it is. Whether damaged or completely shattered, we have the capacity to transform ourselves into something beautiful through our own vision and hard work and often by the grace of God.

There is hope in the once-shattered pieces of our lives and they can be sifted for any remnants of our strength, knowledge and vision. We can craft a special mosaic of what we've salvaged and each one of us will bear a different one that casts a unique light onto the world. As we look upon its one-of-a-kind value, the hope in our future is highlighted clearly and so is our ability to transform.

Like the bright beacon of light that calls a sea captain home, we can be assured that we are safely and lovingly guided when we keep our eyes on that light. What was once broken, in either ourselves or our lives, has the capacity to one day be deemed a masterpiece.

My Journey Continues

When I rely on wisdom there is more to uncover.

S imilar to a blueprint, my first steps on the beach represented the start of a journey conceived out of divine inspiration, knowledge and expertise by my creator – the master architect, who placed my purpose in His plans.

To draw it accurately, a portrayal of my essence was devised. It comprised a lifetime of ups, downs, detours and rest stops. Laughter, tears and happiness were elements, and so were experiences that would either make or try to break me. Countless miles of personally-marked territory showed levels of growth and change. Not every detail was intact because free will leaves room for choices, mistakes and other uncertainties along the way.

Born equipped with the necessities for a life of new and ever-changing possibilities, I look forward to many opportunities and reach out in expectation as much as possible instead of doubt, despite the apprehension that may creep in. I periodically return to God's drafting table for reassurance and strength and am consistently met with patience; one of the things He tries to teach me daily.

I'm not one to rely on wishful thought entirely, but instead try to live with a level of purpose and passion to keep ambitions visible and alive. Purpose won't always arise through a dramatic mission or obvious sign, but it's noticed by living each day with focus for it to be the best it can be.

The accomplishments of anyone, no matter how small or significant, can make a difference in the course of one life or many, providing purpose one step at a time. Life's main goal is not designed to solely benefit oneself; for if so, nothing gained would be shared with others and selfishness may bring a feeling of emptiness.

Real purpose comes about when I live with an awareness that reaches beyond living in a shallow manner.

My life's main objective is more apparent when I continue to move past my current level of comfort and knowledge and also remain diligent by serving myself and others with the best intentions in mind.

The manner in which I proceed in life is accomplished through yearnings, indications and an occasional impulse, and I do my best not to live in neutral gear. My power is only limited by how I limit myself and it's up to me to turn desires into actions and pitfalls into plans so my journey can come full circle.

There's abundance before me and to live and honor life as the grand gift it is helps to grow beyond the place I stand at any given moment. Every day is enough for itself though never includes all of what I hope to do or experience. It seems the more I experience, the more I want, which is what happens when I sit at the surf. I feel the vibrations and stirrings from the inside and that's how I want to experience life.

I never plan to stand still for too long, but there are times I need a push to keep going. Stagnancy dishonors the one who gives me the chance to embrace the gift of life as the greatest one bestowed. To squander or waste it is like locking myself in a dungeon though the sun calls me out to live.

I love myself enough to be truthful no matter what I see in myself or another. I have a private rendezvous with my inner self often, so I'm comfortable with its honesty and experience clarity. By doing so, every moment is a conscious one no matter what they reveal or entail. I'd rather live with eyes wide open than reject the truth. Also, a life only lived in black or white creates limitations and no room for growth. Within the realm of restrictions is also evidence of limited knowledge and a stubborn nature.

Self-discovery has shown me my strengths and weaknesses and I now stand with greater ability on my own while allowing others to do the same for themselves. Helping another shouldn't be about the ability to control or enable, but sometimes be about allowing, accepting and letting go when necessary.

I also realize that change may not be as important as acceptance and to apply either at the right time is to be wise. It's difficult to accept the unacceptable and the unsolved in my life, but the fact remains that perfect fairness or desired outcomes are not guaranteed and there are certain things I can't change no matter how much I wish to do so. Witnessing my own powerlessness in certain situations reminds me of my human nature and removes the pressure to control everything that comes my way.

If acceptance isn't applied in many of life's moments, inner conflict or stress can emerge, thereby creating a blockage to feeling content. The ability to apply acceptance to life can be difficult, but if I don't learn to do so, resistance causes angst or pain. On rare occasions there are things I refuse to embrace if they are hurtful or dangerous; then, an active attempt to change them, if possible, is an option.

Life is meant for growth, not necessarily continual comfort on perfect terrain, and I try to stay the course. I also try to remain focused so there's no need to wonder about what might have been missed or ignored. During moments of hesitation or struggle, there are always other options when the going gets tough or if my will to carry on has diminished. Though an immediate resolution is sometimes far from sight, things usually do have a way of working themselves out for the best.

On the contrary, it's easy to remember and cherish the experiences that have given me immense joy and hope, and I look upon them as a reminder that life hides many wonderful moments behind occasional gloomy skies.

When things are in the way of my path, they're often placed there out of fear, although it may not be apparent at the moment. Other times, challenges pose themselves as interference, but they can be used as a cue to learn how to navigate around them, become resourceful or place myself on the edge of blind trust. No matter where I'm led, faith goes before me in order to stay resilient each day and the determination accumulated paves a way to more endurance.

I'm confident that life's events are part of a grand scheme that often fit perfectly like a puzzle. Each piece later shows that their particular shape or size conformed to my path thus far. Whether huge positive swells or barren lulls dictate my path, I've learned that different experiences are meant specifically for my growth. Sometimes, I end up in a place that's a complete surprise and what was thought to be uncomfortable or unbearable has turned out to suit the outcome and my life precisely.

Despite the decisions made, every lesson helps guide me. With an open mind, I do my best to keep my vision clear by what I believe to be divine guidance. If there are missteps along the way, I try to redirect them on steadier ground in the future.

I'll always embrace my experiences, and as the memories are recalled, try to limit my attachment to any pain associated. Regarding distress or discomfort, they have been weaved into my personal fabric, which is much stronger and reinforced now because of them. Though my lifeboat still holds some baggage and always will, my strength won't be evident unless heavy loads are mine to occasionally carry. However, it's important to remember to throw them overboard when they become too heavy so I don't sink.

Negative situations and especially thoughts of that nature are barriers and I do my best to send them on their way. They're like predators waiting to pounce on a weakened state of mind. To be sharp and resistant to them, I must be aware of how they're fed and am responsible for allowing them to stay. If I don't control or destroy them, I become my own betrayer.

When past mistakes are dredged up, I still know myself to be a beautiful being of light who is sometimes required to navigate through murky waters while being entrenched in confusion or apprehension. I'll also forgive myself for mistakes, hurting others or for unreasonable expectations.

The compassion, love and forgiveness I give are free and they help me become a better person. The price is only the cost of sharing my heart and a bit of humility. The blessings received are most often returned ten-fold, but an occasional person filters into my space with an unkind response or dose of drama. For them, I realize opposition and ignorance will always be part of life and I'm free to control those allowed in my personal space for my best interests.

At times, there's resistance or pain regarding things of the past, but the strain of pushing them away does nothing to change that they are part of me. To purposely focus my energy on removing these things has proven counterproductive or futile most times, as they usually return to jolt me with negative energy from out of nowhere. Instead, I try to patiently accept their presence for what they are, but view them as a reminder that they don't own nor enslave me. By doing so, I can make better sense of things and the purpose they served seems more apparent. They are merely a glimpse into a past that has no power over me unless I allow it.

I'm learning to recollect without regret, yet do my best to make sense of the steps, roadblocks and detours taken if they were detrimental to me or another in any way. Through it all, I've been shown that sometimes the long way home was necessary and the discomfort felt was like the process to refine a raw diamond. When I return to myself after the arduous journey I see the change in the person I've become. Thankfully, the metamorphosis proves positive most often and the reflection back at me is proof of what transpires from being resilient and willing to be placed in the fire of transformation.

Through times of lack, I'm reassured by seagulls when I watch them closely. They search for sustenance in washed up sea life and prove that nature's flow meets my needs when I endure a hunger for life if pushed below the line of certainty. The phrase, "This too shall pass" is true and rising up again brings me higher than the time before, replenished and renewed.

There is more to my physical, emotional and spiritual body as I know it, and behind the scenes of daily life is something much larger than myself. It has been evidenced through the years and I have plans to uncover and retrieve more of life's hidden mysteries. Not everything is as it appears. I remain open to all that has yet to enlighten me and know every day brings me closer to life's golden moments.

I don't have much if I have love without honoring it, health without appreciating it or opportunities without embracing them. The same is true for blessings without noticing them, freedom without using it or wisdom without sharing it. All of this teaches me that most of all I can't embrace life without consciously living it.

I'm like a river that flows continuously toward the ocean, where a vast sea awaits and no dream or destination is too grand to be considered. In order for me to reach for the stars in my own galaxy, I must use a generous dose of reality, a splash of audacity, confidence and a plan to do so.

I'll never be spiritually barren or dead since what resides within me has been sparked to life by a guiding force. My life's desires throb with a need for expression and the passion instilled in me may periodically wane, but I trust it will reignite through strong prompts or inspirations that are impossible to ignore.

Since my wildest dreams and reality have a chance to merge through my own perseverance, God's help, synchronicity or any combination therein, I can be assured it's where the desires of my heart have been placed and that's exactly from where I plan to live.

No longer off the beaten path, I proceed toward my final destiny. I hope to be an instrument of wisdom and love in the lives of others that I hold close to my heart and also to those encountered along the way.

It's as if my life is creating a special song I've yet to hear in its entirety, and I intend to listen closely for every note along the way. Like any music, it can't be seen, but is felt from the inside and stirs much from its slumber. If I stay connected to the tune, there will always be something more to gain by all that awakens inside of me. This song holds little purpose unless I also dance, and while a few of my steps may be out of sync to the music, I'll look past that and simply keep my feet moving to honor my specific journey.

My entire path has assisted and molded me spiritually, yet I'm still not completely who I'm meant to be. I'm anxious to know who God sees standing before Him one day when my journey is complete and the vision He had of me long ago can be seen in whole.

At the end of my days, my collected treasures and bag of broken shells will have had so much personal meaning that physically recounting them won't be necessary. They'll be buried within me for my journey upward and onward. Hopefully, their remnants will be a clear indication that my life wasn't lived in vain and that the manner in which I lived spoke to many people in a positive way, despite my flawed self.

I've walked with good intentions and have done so in my own genuine truth…a gift given to myself because to live an authentic life is important to me. I can rest upon the fact that when my ashes are spread into the ocean, it's really me my loved ones will bid goodbye and not a version I wished for them to know.

While time passes, lessons unfold, and the song of my soul will be nearly complete with a melody fit only for me. That will be the time when I sing with complete freedom and bear a smile and grateful heart that proves I'm overwhelmed by its special tune.

When it's time to stop dancing to the music, the architect of divine wisdom will roll up my plans. My legacy will show proof of a woman who found her soul and her song, both connected to a special source that is hard to ignore.

Thankfully, I learned to listen and became more conscious of my journey, and though not perfect, my life reveals a grateful person who walked with confidence toward her unique and well-lived destiny.

A *promise letter can be a commitment we make regarding the life we wish to live and the manner in which we decide to treat ourselves.*

It's a reminder that although we are flawed and sometimes inconsistent, we should remain open-minded and fully aware that our opinion of ourselves often dictates our level of successes or setbacks.

Everyone's promise letter will be composed in a different way to reflect individual realizations and promises, but when written, is a testament of love and faith that the journey before us and our connection to it is directly linked to how we feel about ourselves and what we believe we deserve out of life. To be our own worst enemy is to sabotage our goals, purpose and personal value.

Though we intimately know our own heart and soul, why not compose your own promise letter? Oftentimes, when we actually see something concrete it has the capacity to resonate much stronger with us and is viewed seriously for its worth because it is highlighted visually.

Following is an example of what you can create or you can use the one on the next page to remind yourself that you are the most important person in your life's journey.

The Promise Letter

From this day forward, I promise to accept and love myself as a beautiful creation of God, though there are times I don't feel worthy. I won't place my worth selfishly above another, but will always realize my own individuality and value.

I'll take any occasional unworthiness felt and replace it with reminders that, though not perfect, I have plenty of traits and God-given gifts deserving of appreciation and recognition.

I leave behind the need to critically and hurtfully judge what I do and say about myself, for it only dulls the radiance of my soul. If improvements need to be made, I'll do so objectively and lovingly, in a manner to uplift instead of destroy.

I choose to stop assuming what others may negatively think of me and replace it with patience for myself regarding the mistakes and weaknesses of being human. I will also curtail the assumptions I have about others when I am tempted to view them as fact, and know that I can never know all unless I have witnessed their journey.

If someone else judges me negatively, it is their interpretation, not my own, nor is it necessarily the truth. Any incorrect assumptions are often a misunderstanding of who I am at my core and they're not aware of prior experiences or reasons pertaining to my actions. If I am met with the negative truths, it's my choice to determine how to deal with them and always try to consider others when doing so.

My inner thoughts and feelings may not always be relatable to another because they haven't walked with me in the direction my life has taken. Until they do, they won't truly grasp my intentions or reasons.

Another's view of me is not a defining factor regarding my authenticity or value as a person; it's only a sampling of the actions they've witnessed and may reveal only a small amount of truth regarding everything I am on a whole. In the same way, I will offer graces to another simply because they are human as well, unless their goal is to defile or destroy.

I'll take all of my experiences, whether good, bad or challenging and extract what resonates with me in order to understand and use it for the ultimate good of myself and others.

I'll put all of life's hurtful experiences in their proper resting place where they deserve to be, instead of continually exposing them for further interrogation and unnecessary dissection. Once I've come to terms or healed them, revealing them continually causes

131

unnecessary discomfort or pain. Their lessons, memories or purpose shall instead be recalled to provide a reminder of my strength and amazing growth.

My actions through recounting events in my life shall remain those of purpose and the experiences will no longer carry the weight of any guilt I assigned, for it only serves to lessen the love and tranquility in my heart and soul. Most importantly, these events remembered will show I am imperfect but can still learn, decipher, embrace, accept and let go on a daily basis if I desire a life of peace.

I'll start each day with a clear, new outlook in order to continue on a path of spiritual growth while accepting my humanness. Though my flaws remain, I will try not to enmesh them with the fabric of my being nor bring attention to them in a way that berates me.

Instead of fear, which can immobilize, I'll use wonder and hope. These fuel desire and desire sparks action.

If negative thoughts creep inward to rattle me, I'll divert or change them instead of focus on them, since how I think is often the reality I create. I'll treat worry and insecurity as distractions and know they only serve to provide confusion and imbalance in my life.

I'll try my best to release the past and wash it away with forgiveness for its mistakes, compassion for its pain, understanding for its imperfections and gratitude for its pleasures. I'll greet my future days as opportunities to help myself while helping others.

Each new day promises a beautiful gift and I will open each one with self-love, a receptive mind, an eager spirit and most of all, gratitude.

*E*mbrace the ocean from wherever you are with these beautiful, ocean-related quotes:

"Your heart is the size of an ocean. Go find yourself in its hidden depths."
Rumi

"There is nothing more beautiful than the way the ocean refuses to stop kissing the shoreline, no matter how many times it's sent away."
Sarah Kay

"Wherever people go to find peace, that's what I've found in the ocean."
Willow Aster

"The voice of the sea speaks to the soul. The touch of the sea is sensuous, enfolding the body in its soft, close embrace."
Kate Chopin

"For whatever we lose, it's always ourselves we find at the sea."
E.E. Cummings

"I can never stay long enough on the shore; the tang of the untainted, fresh and free sea air was like a cool, quieting thought."

Helen Keller

"Should you ever feel too lonely...listen for the roar of the sea, for in it are all those who've been and all those who are to come."
Simon Van Booy

"When I walk down the beach and smell the salt water, hear the waves crashing against the shoreline and feel the granular sand under my feet, I can't help but realize why I am here on this green earth."
Wendy Joubert

"Tell me once more about the eternal surf."
Rob Bignell

"He was beneath the waves, a creature crawling the ocean bottom."
Doppo Kunikida

"Why does the ocean rock the moon to sleep every night? So the sun will wake and kiss the beach."
J. Henson

"To myself I am only a child playing on the beach, while vast oceans of truth lie undiscovered before me."
Isaac Newton

"Can we fathom the ocean, dark and deep, where the mighty waves and the grandeur sweep?"
Fanny Crosby

"My soul is full of longing for the secrets of the sea, and the heart of the great ocean sends a thrilling pulse through me."
Henry Wadsworth Longfellow

"The sea, once it casts its spell, holds one in its net of wonder forever."
Jacques Yves Cousteau

"A lot of people attack the sea. I make love to it."
Jacques Yves Cousteau

"I dropped a tear in the ocean and whenever they find it, I'll stop loving you, only then."
Anonymous

"The voice of the sea speaks to the soul. The touch of the sea is sensuous, enfolding the body in its soft, close embrace."
Kate Chopin

"Once your feet have touched the warm, sun-drenched sand of the seashore, you will never be the same."
Pasty Gant

"The sea does not reward those who are too anxious, too greedy or too impatient. One should lie empty, open, choiceless as a beach — waiting for a gift from the sea."
Ann Morrow Lindberg

"I shall listen to the language of your soul, as the shore listens to the story of the waves."
Khalil Gibran

"For whatever we lose (like a you or a me) it's always ourselves that we find in the sea."
E.E. Cummings

"The ocean stirs the heart, inspires the imagination and brings eternal joy to the soul."
Wyland

"After a visit to the beach, it's hard to believe that we live in a material world."
Pam Shaw

"The cure for anything is salt water, sweat, tears or the sea."
Isak Dinesen

"Eternity begins and ends with the ocean's tides."
Anonymous

"A woman's heart is a deep ocean of secrets."
Gloria Stuart

"Individually, we are a drop. Together, we are an ocean."
Ryunosuke Satoro

"Man cannot discover new oceans unless he has the courage to lose sight of the shore."
Andre Gide

"Our memories of the ocean will linger on, long after our footprints in the sand are gone."
Anonymous

"Writers begin with a grain of sand, and then create a beach."
Robert Black

"You've been walking the ocean's edge, holding up your robes to keep them dry. You must dive naked under and deeper under, a thousand times deeper."
Rumi

"From birth, man carries the weight of gravity on his shoulders. He is bolted to earth. But man has only to sink beneath the surface and he is free."
Jacques Yves Cousteau

"The sea is everything. It covers seven tenths of the terrestrial globe. Its breath is pure and healthy. It is an immense desert, where man is never lonely, for he feels life stirring on all sides."
Jules Verne

"And forget not that the earth delights to feel your bare feet and the winds love to play with your hair."
Kahlil Gibran

"I've found it...Eternity. It's the sun mingled with the sea."
Arthur Rimbaud

15511933R00089

Made in the USA
Middletown, DE
08 November 2014